COUNTRY QUILTING

McCall's Needlework & Crafts

MEREDITH® PRESS
New York

DEAR QUILTER:

Thank you for selecting COUNTRY QUILTING, one of three
books in a series developed by *McCall's Needlework & Crafts*
magazine. COUNTRY QUILTING is packed with inventive and
instructive ideas inviting you to construct a colorful variety of quilt
projects.

An assortment of 15 country coordinates takes you from the
kitchen to the bedroom to the living area to the children's
playroom. One hundred applique patterns offer numerous
decorative possibilities that range from the formal to the witty.

We at Meredith Press are dedicated to bringing you craft books
that you will refer to time after time. All of the popular projects are
enhanced by full-color photographs, large, easy-to-trace patterns,
detailed instructions, and comprehensive sections on the latest
techniques. COUNTRY QUILTING will guide you to the most
beautiful and distinctive results possible!

Sincerely,

Connie Schrader

The Editors

Meredith ® Press is an imprint of Meredith ® Books:

President, Book Group: Joseph J. Ward
Vice President. Editorial Director: Elizabeth P. Rice

For Meredith Press:

Executive Editor: Connie Schrader
Project Manager: Barbara Machtiger
Project Editor: Gloria Mosesson
Editorial Assistants: Valerie Martone and Carolyn Mitchell
Production Manager: Bill Rose

ISBN: 0-696-02352-0 (hard cover)
ISBN: 0-696-02372-5 (trade paperback)
Library of Congress Card Number: 90-063671

Packaged by Rapid Transcript, a division of March Tenth, Inc.
Design by Stanley S. Drate/Folio Graphics Co., Inc.

Printed in the United States of America
10 9 8 7 6 5 4 3 2 1

CONTENTS

Introduction / 5

DECORATIVE ACCENTS

Floral Shadows / 7
Star Flower Table Runner / 11
Sitting Pretty Sewing Machine Cover / 14
Capture a Snowflake / 16
Take Time for Tea / 19
Country Coordinates / 24

PILLOWS AND QUILTS: A WARM TRADITION

Pretty Pillows / 28
Red and White Pattern Play / 32
Autumn Leaves / 39
Appliqué Pussycat / 43

JUNIOR ATTRACTIONS

Nursery Pals / 47
Cat and Mouse / 54
Snacktime Treats / 57
Garden Bunnies / 61
Quilt Block Fun / 64

Quilting Compendium / 69

Source Guide / 77

Index / 79

INTRODUCTION

No one knows exactly when some creative and practical ancestor or ancestors of modern man realized that layers of fabric provide more warmth than one heavy garment or covering. Then these clever people realized that something had to hold these layers together, perhaps joining them at their borders and later in their centers—in other words, quilting.

There has never been a human generation that did not try to invest beauty and symbolism into everyday objects. Quilting represents both goals, for we seem to have no samples of quilts or quilted objects or clothing that do not demonstrate this. For example, that most plebian of quilted objects, the bed cover, has graduated from its original function of providing maximum warmth with minimum weight to a thing of beauty incorporating a high degree of craftsmanship and meaning.

The stitching can be intricate and the fabric pieces joined in patchwork (with which quilting is often combined) to provide visual attractiveness. But the special thing about quilts is that they so often have real symbolism, real meaning in a community or a family or to an individual. Their patterns were (and are) often traditional, handed down through generations and regarded as special for weddings, births, and other important occasions, including community events. They even marked milestones in wars and exploration.

Earlier generations that did not have the advantages of central heating cherished quilts for their practicality. Today, we do, too, but they have become decorative objects as well. We hang antique and modern quilts, and we make more that we hope will be treasured by our descendants. Just as in other areas we've broken many of our links with the past, we have taken the freedom to experiment with new uses for this ancient craft.

So in this book of projects we not only go far afield from traditional patterns in bed quilts, but we've adapted the technique to a whole new range of objects—some purely practical that we've made pretty as well, and some that say, "Admire me. I'm handsome and different."

In the pages that follow, you'll find quilting projects for almost every room in any home, for almost any age level from newborn to senior citizen, for men and women, and for tastes from tailored to elaborate.

Each is a challenge, not only in terms of workmanship, but with respect to imagination and creativity. Yours will be the eye that selects the colors, chooses the design and fabric, and decides on the uses of your handiwork.

Enjoy!

DECORATIVE ACCENTS

How often have you admired a room or an entire home and then realized that what made it so attractive was not the furniture or the room size, but all the accessories—the special touches that loaned individuality to the setting? Here is a selection of quilted "touches" that can help you put your special imprint on your home, or let you dress up someone else's environment with a gift that says, "Just for you!"

Floral Shadows

Here is a selection of pretty and practical accessories that will find a place in any home. Combine shadow quilting with painted design for a mixed-media set that includes picture frame, tissue-box cover, tote bag, and small planter . . . or make them individually in a variety of nonmatching fabrics and colors.

EQUIPMENT: Ruler. Pencil. Paper for patterns. Dressmaker's tracing (carbon) paper. Dry ball-point pen. Blotting paper. Scissors. Straight pins. Sewing and embroidery needles. Sewing machine. Steam iron.

MATERIALS (for each): Closely woven white cotton fabric 45″ wide.* White voile 44″ wide.* White pregathered eyelet edging ¾″ and 1½″ wide.* Vogart™ ball-point paint: one tube each 1902 yellow, 1907 rose, 1914 medium green, 1915 forest green, 1917 light blue, 1919 violet. Batting.* White six-strand embroidery floss, one skein. White sewing thread.

*See individual directions for amounts and for any additional materials.

GENERAL DIRECTIONS: Review "Quilting Compendium," page 69–76. Draw lines across patterns given here, connecting grid lines. Enlarge patterns by copying on paper ruled in 1″ squares. Following individual directions, use dressmaker's carbon and dry ball-point pen to transfer patterns to white cotton fabric.

Place marked fabric right side up on work surface with a sheet of blotting paper underneath. Fill in designs with paint, following color key and paint manufacturer's directions; paint all small dots yellow; let dry.

Cut out each painted design as directed. Cut a matching piece of voile and a piece of batting ¼″ smaller all around. Pin voile over painted cotton; pin batting, centered, underneath. Using three strands of embroidery floss in needle, work backstitches (see page 74) around each painted shape and along inner edge of border bands.

Assemble pieces following individual directions. Sew pieces together with right sides facing, edges even, and making ¼″ seams, unless otherwise directed.

SMALL PLANTER

SIZE: 3¾″ tall.

MATERIALS: Cotton fabric, one piece each 6″ × 13¾″ and 5″ square. Voile, 6″ × 13¾″. Batting, 3¾ × 13¼″. Any empty can 3¼″ tall with a 4″ diameter.

DIRECTIONS: Read General Directions for Floral Shadows. Transfer pattern for tissue box side, centered to white fabric strip; extend border bands the length of the fabric and omit both shorter end bands. Paint design.

Pin voile over and batting under painted piece; work backstitches. Trim long bottom edge ¼″ outside border band. Using can as pattern, lightly mark a 4″-diameter circle on cotton square. Cut out circle ¼″ outside marked line. Sew short ends of painted section together. Pin bottom edge of painted section around fabric circle; stitch together. Turn planter cover right side out. Fold long upper edge to wrong side along top edge of upper border band. Tack folded edge to batting, being careful not to stitch through to front. Place can in planter cover.

PICTURE FRAME

SIZE: 5¼″ × 7¼″.

MATERIALS: Cotton fabric, 7½″ × 9½″. Voile, 7½″ × 9½″. Batting, 5¼″ × 7¼″. Stiff cardboard, one piece each 5″ × 7″ and 5¼″ × 7¼″. Eyelet, ¾″ wide, 28″ length. Double-faced and regular masking tape. Self-stick picture hanger.

DIRECTIONS: Read General Directions for Floral Shadows. Transfer pattern for picture frame, centered, to larger cotton fabric piece. Paint design.

Cut out inner oval ½″ inside oval line. Transfer oval shape to center of voile piece; cut out voile oval ½″ inside oval line. Transfer oval shape to center of larger cardboard and batting pieces; cut out each oval on marked line.

Pin voile over and batting under painted piece; work backstitches. Clip into excess fabric inside oval. Place larger cardboard piece behind fabric layers, fold fabric edges through cardboard oval, and tape fabric edges to back of cardboard. Slipstitch (see page 74) bound edge of eyelet all around frame front along outer edge of border band. Place double-faced tape around back of larger cardboard along sides and bottom. Center smaller cardboard behind frame front and press in place. Attach hanger to back of frame. Insert picture into top of frame.

TISSUE-BOX COVER

SIZE: 5″ × 10½″ × 3¾″ high, plus ruffles.

MATERIALS: Cotton fabric, ⅜ yard. Voile, ⅜ yard. Batting, ¼ yard. Eyelet, ¾″ wide, 1½-yard length.

DIRECTIONS: Read General Directions for Floral Shadows. From white cotton fabric, cut two side pieces, each 4½″ × 11¼″; two end pieces, each 4½″ × 5¾″; and one top piece, 5¾″ × 11¼″. Transfer

Top

PICTURE FRAME

Side

TISSUE-BOX COVER

End

TOTE FRONT/BACK

1 square = 1 inch

1—Yellow
2—Rose
3—Medium green
4—Forest green
5—Light blue
6—Violet

tissue-box patterns, centered, to each piece. Paint designs.

Cut a matching piece of voile and a piece of batting ¾" smaller all around for each painted piece. Transfer inner oval border edge from top pattern to center of corresponding voile and batting pieces. Cut a slit along center of oval on each top piece; clip into curved ends.

Pin voile over and batting under each painted piece. Fold fabric inside oval band on top piece to wrong side; fold bottom edge of each side and end to wrong side along bottom of border band. Pin raw edges to back. Work backstitches, being sure to catch all raw fabric edges.

Pin bound edge of eyelet along each edge of top piece and along both sides of each end piece, so that ruffles face center of each piece with bound edge along outer edge of border band; baste eyelet to fabric. Pin upper edge of each side to long sides of top piece; pin top of each end piece to short sides of top. Sew pieces together, making ¾" seam. Sew side and end pieces together in same way. Remove basting thread. Place cover over an opened tissue box.

TOTE BAG

S I Z E: 9¾" × 11½" × 2".

M A T E R I A L S: Cotton fabric, 1 yard. Voile, ⅓ yard. Batting, ⅓ yard.

D I R E C T I O N S: Review "General Directions for Floral Shadows," page 8. From white cotton fabric, cut two 2½" × 12" bottom gussets, four 2½" × 10¼" side gussets, two 10¼" × 12" lining front/back pieces, and one 4½" × 27" strap; transfer two complete patterns, for front and back, to remaining fabric, leaving at least ½" between squares. Paint design on front and back pieces. When dry, cut out pieces ¼" outside marked lines.

From voile, cut two pieces each same size as painted front and back; from batting, cut one bottom gusset, two side gussets, and two pieces for front and back, all the same size as the cotton pieces. Pin voile over and batting under each painted piece; work backstitches.

Join one end of each cotton side gusset to short ends of cotton bottom gussets; repeat with batting gussets, for a total of three strips. Pin batting gusset strip to wrong side of one fabric gusset strip. Pin and sew this strip around side and bottom edges of painted front piece, matching seams with corners of front piece. Pin and sew other long edge of same gusset strip to painted back piece. Turn tote right side out. Press raw upper edges ¼" to wrong side. For lining, join remaining gusset strip to remaining cotton front and back pieces in same manner. Do not turn right side out. Press raw top edges ¼" to wrong side.

Fold strap in half lengthwise. Sew long edges together; turn right side out and press. Pin each raw strap end to wrong side of each side gusset on tote, so that strap ends are ½" below upper folded edges. Using three strands of white embroidery floss, take small running stitches (see page 74) across strap, ¼" from each end, securing strap to tote. Place lining in tote. Slip-stitch upper folded edges together all around.

Star Flower Table Runner

This country appliqué table runner creates a mirror image in shades of pink and red with two full-blown star flowers and four ready-to-open buds. Quilters will delight in the combination of patchwork, appliqué, and quilting.

SIZE: 12″ × 40″.

MATERIALS: Cotton calicoes 44″ wide: ½ yard navy, ¼ yard aqua, plus scraps of cherry pink, dark rust, and rose. Navy broadcloth 44″ wide, ⅜ yard. White and navy threads.

DIRECTIONS: Review "Quilting Compendium," pages 69–76. Prepare patterns for leaves 2 and 3 as directed. Runner is composed of two lily-and-bud blocks with a strip of background fabric. Stem and leaves are appliquéd after piecing.

Lily Design: Patches: Trace diamond patterns A

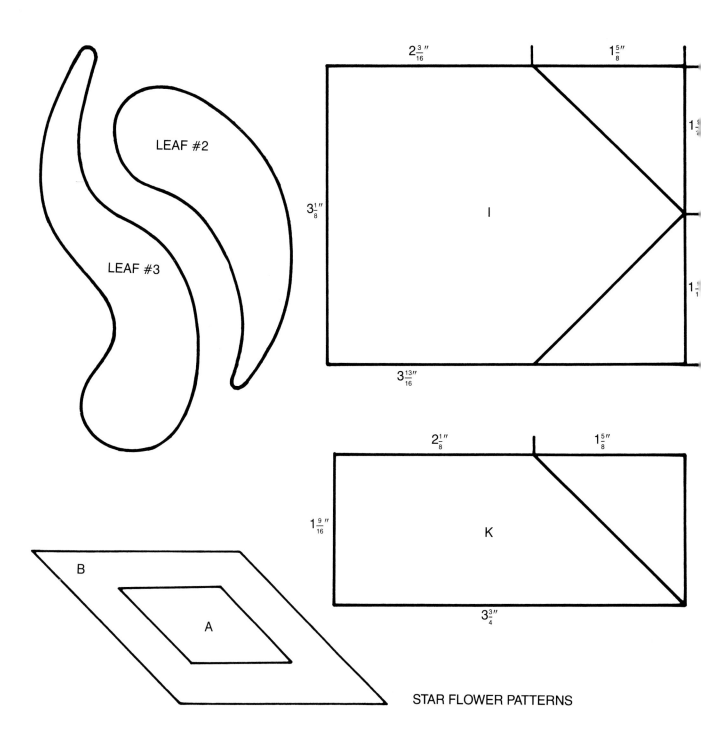

LEAF #2

LEAF #3

$2\frac{3}{16}''$ $1\frac{5}{8}''$

$3\frac{1}{8}''$

I

$3\frac{13}{16}''$

$2\frac{1}{8}''$ $1\frac{5}{8}''$

$1\frac{9}{16}''$

K

$3\frac{3}{4}''$

STAR FLOWER PATTERNS

B

A

and B; make into templates. Before cutting patches, test each template on paper by marking around it eight times to make an eight-pointed star. If there are any gaps or overlaps between diamonds, remake templates until they are accurate. Make additional templates of other patches, marking dimensions on graph paper: C—2¼" square. H—4⁷⁄₁₆" square. I—see diagram. J—2¼" × 4⅜" rectangle. K—see diagram. Cut patches, adding ¼" seam allowances:

From pink, cut 28 A.
From rust, cut 18 A.
From rose, cut 6 A.
From aqua, cut 12 A and 4 B.
From navy, cut 2 C, 4 H, 6 I, 4 J, and 4 K.

Piecing: Join twenty-four pink A's to a rust or rose A to make a two-patch row. Join each pink/rose row to a pink/rust row to make a diamond-shaped A petal with pink patches at center of the petal (see shaded

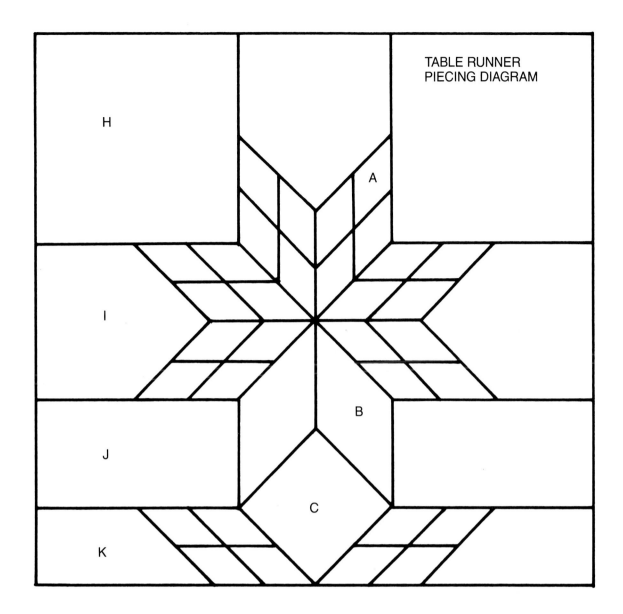

A's on Piecing Diagram). In same manner, join remaining pink/rust rows to each other with pink patches at center of diamond. Join each remaining pink A to an aqua A. Join remaining aqua A's to each other in two-patch rows. Join pink/aqua and all-aqua rows to make four A buds (see Piecing Diagram).

To make each end block, arrange six A petals and two B patches, placing rust patches at center of lily. Fill in edges with H, I, J, and C patches. Stitch A petals and B patches together in pairs to make four sections. Add H and J patches. Join sections, then add I and C patches. Join each A bud to a K patch, then join to block. Block should measure 11⅞" × 12½", including seam allowance around edges. Make two end blocks.

From navy fabric, cut piece 12½" × 17¾". Stitch end blocks to each short edge of navy piece in ¼" seams. Runner should measure 12½" × 40½".

Appliqué: Make templates for leaf patterns 2 and 3. Following directions, cut four of each leaf from aqua fabric, reversing template for two of each. For stem, cut cardboard strip ⅜" × 12". From aqua fabric, cut ⅞" × 24" straight-grain strip. Place fabric strip wrong side up. Working in stages, place cardboard strip at center, then fold long edges onto cardboard and press; remove cardboard. At one end of aqua strip, fold corners to wrong side, forming a right-angle point; press. Pin stem on runner as shown, fitting point to B patches of one lily. Slip-stitch stem in place, beginning at fitted end; trim and fit opposite end. Appliqué leaves as shown.

Finishing: From broadcloth, cut piece 12½" × 40½". Place top and lining with right sides together. Stitch ¼" seam, leaving an opening for turning. Trim corners, turn, and slip-stitch opening closed. Press runner.

Sitting Pretty Sewing Machine Cover

Cat fanciers will appreciate this crafty sewing machine cover. Calico appliqué on face and tail add a touch of warmth to the white quilted body of this friendly feline dustcover.

SIZE: 15″ × 10″ (see directions).

MATERIALS: White quilted fabric 45″ wide, ½ yard (see directions). White broadcloth, piece 9″ × 9″. Small pieces of black, rust, and tan broadcloth and dark yellow satin. Heavy fusible interfacing, ¼ yard. Pellon® Wonder-Under™ Transfer Fusing Web. Pellon® Stitch-n-Tear®. Matching sewing thread. Fiberfill.

DIRECTIONS: Review "Quilting Compendium," pages 69–76. Enlarge body and appliqué patterns.

Body pattern as given will fit front and back of a 15″-long, 10″-high sewing machine; there is a 3½″-wide gusset joining body pieces. Measure sewing machine to be covered and adjust body pattern piece at dot/dash lines to fit machine. Additional fabric may be required to accommodate pattern adjustments. From quilted fabric, cut two body pieces and two tail pieces, adding ½″ seam allowance all around. Also cut strip for gusset in length and width required, allowing for ½″ seam allowance.

1 square = 1 inch

Appliqués: Trace outline of cat face onto heavy fusible interfacing; fuse to wrong side of white broadcloth following manufacturer's directions. Cut out face along traced line. Trace features onto tissue paper. *Reverse tissue* and, using dressmaker's carbon and dry ball-point pen, trace features onto paper side of transfer web; label sections. Cut features apart along marked lines. Place web side of all features on *wrong* side of appropriate color fabric. Press with hot iron for three seconds to fuse; allow to cool. Cut along lines and remove paper backing. Position pieces on broadcloth side of a cat face, omitting eyes. Fuse in place with iron for ten seconds; allow to cool. Cut and fuse calico tail pieces in similar manner. Set sewing machine for ⅛" satin stitch and stitch around each appliqué piece on cat face and tail with matching thread. Center face on 11"×11" piece of Stitch-n-Tear®. Set sewing machine for ³⁄₁₆" satin stitch and stitch face outline and mouth and ear details with black thread. Also

stitch front paws and haunch on one cat body, for front. Using ¼" satin stitch and black thread, appliqué eyes. Stitch over center of eyelids with white. Remove excess Stitch-n-Tear®.

Assembly: Sew tail pieces together, leaving straight end open. Trim seams, clip curves, and turn right side out; stuff with fiberfill. Pin tail to front with open end at side edge between dots; baste in place. To reinforce seams, cut two strips of heavy fusible interfacing ¾" wide and as long as gusset. Fuse to wrong side of gusset, matching each strip to a long edge. With right sides together, stitch gusset to body front along sides and top with ½" seam, easing at curves. Repeat with body back. Clip seams at curves and press toward gusset. Turn bottom edge 1" to inside and blindstitch in place. Turn machine cover right side out. Position cat face on front; tack to body at chin and forehead. Tack tail to body above curve in tail.

Capture a Snowflake

Snowflake wall hangings that reflect the winter season are an especially delightful form of Christmas decor—and attractive all year round. Stenciling the design is easy. You can make your own snowflake variations after you've tried the ones here.

SIZES: About 14¾" and 18¾", finished.

EQUIPMENT: Ruler. Small, sharp paper scissors. Tissue or tracing paper. Pencil. Protractor. White freezer paper. Straight pins. Iron. Plastic drop cloth or old newspapers. Masking tape. Small, soft cosmetic sponge. Cup or small bowl. Press cloth. Sewing and quilting needles. Shears. Fine sandpaper. Small paintbrush and stencil brush (optional).
For blue hoop: Water-erasable marking pen or tailor's chalk.

MATERIALS: Wooden quilting hoop with tension screw, 1" deep × 14" or 18" diameter. Unbleached muslin, two squares 6" larger than diameter of hoop purchased. Matching sewing thread. Acrylic paint or stencil paint for fabric. Quilt batting. Acrylic varnish.

DIRECTIONS: Cutting Patterns: Cut a square of tissue or tracing paper the same size as the diameter of hoop to be used. Fold paper, following Folding Diagrams: **Figure 1:** Fold square in half for rectangle. **Figure 2:** Fold rectangle in half for small square. Use protractor and ruler to mark off square into thirds as shown by dash lines. **Figure 3:** Fold up bottom corner of small square as shown. **Figure 4:** Turn piece over. **Figure 5:** Fold down top corner, meeting opposite edge. Mark small X near tip of segment made. Unfold paper; there will be twelve segments marked by fold lines. Place segments marked with X over large or small motif and trace. Refold paper to twelve thicknesses and cut out shaded areas on pattern, through folded sides only; leave open ends intact. Unfold piece and smooth it as flat as possible. Check to be sure design is the

16

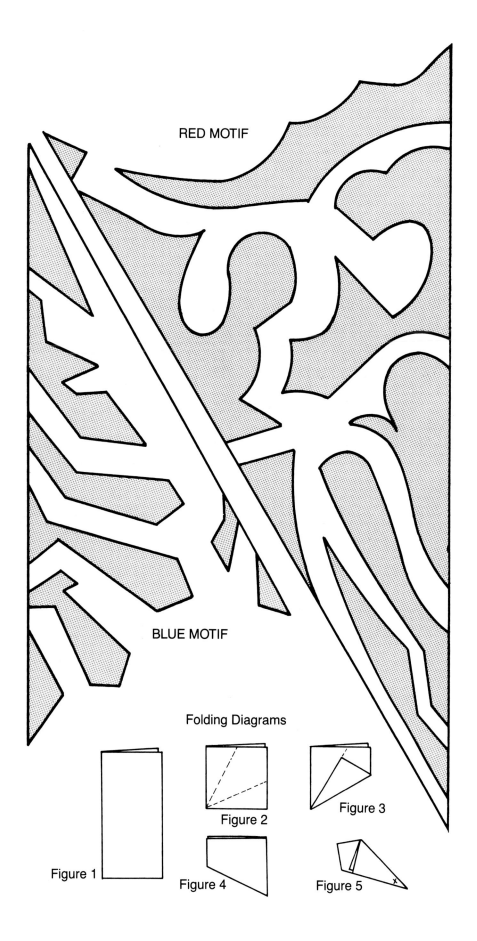

RED MOTIF

BLUE MOTIF

Folding Diagrams

Figure 1

Figure 2

Figure 3

Figure 4

Figure 5

same all around. Experiment with your own cutting designs, if desired. When you are satisfied with your technique, fold and cut a same-size square of freezer paper in the same manner.

Stenciling: Press one muslin square smooth; center unfolded stencil on muslin, shiny side of paper toward fabric. Use a hot iron to tack paper to muslin, beginning at center and moving out and around. When stencil is smooth on muslin, use more pressure to make sure all edges are securely attached to fabric; let piece cool undisturbed.

Arrange drop cloth or newspapers to cover work surface. Tape edges of muslin to surface, with fabric taut and stencil side up. Place several tablespoonfuls of paint into cup or small bowl. Dip sponge into paint and draw it against side of cup to remove excess. Gently smooth sponge over fabric and stencil, being careful not to loosen edges of stencil. Let paint dry a few hours before peeling off paper. If you desire a mottled effect, lightly dab a contrasting color of paint over first color once it has dried. Clean equipment with soap and water as soon as you have finished using it. When paint is thoroughly dry (24–48 hours), press fabric on both sides with a hot iron and press cloth, to set paint.

Quilting: Lay remaining muslin square on work surface; top with batting, then stenciled muslin, right side up. Match edges, then baste layers together securely. Starting at center and working around and outward, quilt along edges of stenciled areas (see quilting stitch detail on page 74). On blue design, use ruler and water-erasable marking pen or tailor's chalk to connect opposite points of design, marking a total of six lines and skipping over stenciled areas. Quilt along lines, then remove markings. Remove basting threads.

Assembling: Lightly sand hoop to remove any waxy or glossy finish. Paint hoop to match motif, or as desired. When paint is dry, apply varnish, following manufacturer's directions. Center snowflake in hoop, placing one point of design at center of screw adjustment area; tighten hoop.

On back side, trim backing and batting even with back edge of hoop. Trim front layer of muslin 1½" from back of hoop, then fold raw edge ¾" toward back of work. Thread needle with doubled thread and make a row of running stitches close to the folded edge. Pull stitching to gather edge evenly; secure thread.

Take Time for Tea

Plan a tea party and match the decor to go with the relaxing teatime ritual. Piece and appliqué a kitchen-cozy wall quilt and coordinating pot holders that can double as hot pads.

SIZES: Quilt, 35″ square; pot holders, 8½″ square.

EQUIPMENT: Paper for patterns. Pencil. Ruler. Scissors. Dressmaker's tracing (carbon) paper. Dry ball-point pen. Sewing and embroidery needles. Sewing machine.

MATERIALS: For quilt: Closely woven cotton fabric 45″ wide (see color photograph for colors or choose your own color scheme): Small print for border and binding, 1½ yards; second small print for lattice, ½ yard; four prints or solids for appliqués, ⅜ yard each, plus scraps in related colors.

White muslin 44" wide, 1½ yards (includes backing). Quilt batting, 35" square. Sewing thread to match fabrics. Six-strand embroidery floss; see individual directions for colors. **For each pot holder:** Gingham fabric with small or medium checks, ¼ yard. Closely woven cotton fabric: solid white, 6½" square; scraps of one solid and one print to match gingham. Quilt batting, two 8½" squares. Sewing thread to match fabrics.

GENERAL DIRECTIONS: Review "Quilting Compendium," pages 69–76. Wash and dry all fabrics; press fabrics, then cut off selvages. Cut fabric pieces as directed below. Sew pieces together with right sides facing, edges even, and making ¼" seams, unless otherwise indicated. Use matching or contrasting sewing thread as desired. Use pencil and ruler to draw lines across appliqué patterns, connecting grid lines; enlarge patterns by copying on paper ruled in 1" squares. On patterns, heavy lines are outlines of pieces; fine lines indicate embroidery. Transfer pattern lines to fabrics with dressmaker's carbon and dry ball-point pen.

QUILT

DIRECTIONS: Review "Quilting Compendium," pages 69–76.

Appliqués: From white muslin, cut one 35" square, for backing; also cut four 10½" squares and four 5½" squares. Set backing piece aside. Enlarge and transfer outlines of a teapot or tea kettle to center of each larger muslin square; transfer outlines of a cup and saucer to center of each smaller square. Following color photograph or as desired, cut appliqué pieces from fabrics as directed in "How to Appliqué," page 75; transfer embroidery lines to appliqué pieces. Following directions for hand-appliqué, baste and sew pieces to muslin squares: **For teapots:** Place spouts, handles, and pedestals beneath teapots; place lids and decorative bands on top of teapots. **For cups and saucers:** Place saucers, pedestals, handles, and inside rims beneath cups; place decorative bands on top of cups.

Work embroidery in outline stitch, using two strands of floss; choose floss colors to coordinate with appliqués.

Quilt top: From one small print, cut fabric strips for lattice, all 2" wide: two A strips, each 10½" long; three B strips, each 22" long; four C strips, each 5½" long; two D strips, each 35" long. From other small print, cut four border pieces, each 5½" × 22". Following diagram, sew a large appliquéd block to each side of one lattice strip A; place teapots as

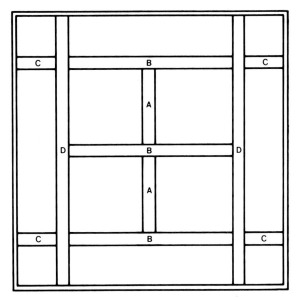

TAKE TIME FOR TEA QUILT
ASSEMBLY DIAGRAM

desired or as shown in color photograph. Sew remaining large blocks to second lattice strip A. Sew block assemblies to each side of one lattice strip B. Sew remaining two lattice strips B to top and bottom of center block assembly. Sew two border pieces (top and bottom) to outer lattice strips B. Sew lattice strips D to sides of assembly. Sew each smaller appliquéd block to lattice strip C, placing cups in the corner closest to their matching pots (see color photograph). Sew strips to bottom or top edge of blocks as shown. Sew other side of each lattice strip C to remaining border pieces (sides). Sew side assemblies to center block assembly. Press all seams toward lattice strips.

Quilting: Measure and mark a point 10¾" from short ends of each border piece, for centers. Enlarge floral quilting pattern as for appliqués; complete half pattern, indicated by dash line. Transfer one complete flower to center of each border piece; stems should point down on top and bottom borders and toward center on side borders. Transfer two more flowers to each side of each center flower, so that leaf tips just meet.

Place muslin backing piece on work surface, right side down. Place batting, then quilt top, right side up on backing with edges even. Baste through all layers lengthwise, crosswise, and diagonally in both directions. Using white thread, quilt by hand or by machine through all layers: Stitch around each appliqué, on lattice strips ¼" in from each long edge, and on border floral pattern.

Finishing: For binding, cut 1¼"-wide strips from same fabric used for border pieces; join strips until length reaches 144". Press each long edge ¼" to wrong side; unfold one edge. Pin binding around

1 square = 1 inch

quilt top with raw edges even and right sides facing, so that binding rests on quilt top. Sew binding to quilt by hand or by machine, stitching on fold line, mitering corners, and overlapping ends. Fold binding over raw quilt edges and slip-stitch folded edge to quilt back.

POT HOLDERS

DIRECTIONS: Review "Quilting Compendium," pages 69–76. From gingham, cut two 9" squares and a 1½" × 6" hanging loop. Enlarge appliqué pattern as for quilt appliqués. Transfer appliqué outlines to center of white cotton square. Following directions for appliqué (see page 75), cut appliqué pieces from fabric scraps as desired or as shown in color photograph. Machine-appliqué pieces to white square, then machine-appliqué white square to center of one gingham square, completing pot holder front.

Fold long edges of gingham hanging loop piece ¼" to wrong side; press. Fold strip in half lengthwise and topstitch ⅛" in from folded edges. Fold strip in half crosswise, matching raw ends. Pin raw ends to top edge of pot holder front at upper left corner, so that loop rests on front piece; baste. Place pot holder front right side up on work surface. Place second gingham square, right side down, then both batting squares, on front piece. Sew layers together all around, catching in ends of hanging loop and leaving an opening for turning at bottom. Turn pot holder right side out; fold raw edges in and slip-stitch opening closed. Remove basting thread.

FLORAL QUILTING PATTERN

1 square = 1 inch

TEA KETTLES QUILT

FLORAL QUILTING PATTERN

1 square = 1 inch

23

Country Coordinates

Kitchens are perhaps second only to bedrooms in their popular use of fabric accessories. Using traditional appliqué patterns, create a kitchen ensemble of complementary place mats, cookbook markers, a bun warmer, and a calendar holder.

MATERIALS: Thread in white, peach, blue gray, and teal. Batting. Calico fabrics 45″ wide: white with peach mini-print (A), blue-gray with large floral (B), blue-gray with small floral (C), peach with small floral (D), peach mini-floral (E), peach plaid (F), peach with large floral (G), light green (H), teal (I). See individual directions for fabric amounts and additional materials.

GENERAL DIRECTIONS: Review "Quilting Compendium," pages 69–76. To appliqué, trace actual-size patterns and create other patterns as indicated. Reverse pattern pieces for half of the upper

and lower leaf sections, buds, and curved stems. Transfer design outlines to appropriate fabrics and cut out. Following directions and referring to color photograph for placement, arrange appliqués on backgrounds. Allow lower leaf section to overlap upper leaf section slightly. Place flower center on flower cup and center both on flower petals section. Fuse and stitch using a narrow zigzag setting.

To add cording, pin cording around appliquéd front, with raw edges matching and ends overlapping and "disappearing" into seam allowance in a corner or inside curve. Baste around, either by hand or using zipper foot to get as close as possible to cord.

small amounts of B, D, H, and I. Wood dowel ⅜" in diameter, 14½" length. Twine.

DIRECTIONS: From fabric E, cut two 14" × 40" (includes ½" seam allowance) rectangles for background and backing. For circular vine, mark circles with a 4¼" radius and a 4½" radius having the same center on a sheet of paper. Pattern is area between circles. Use pattern to cut vine from I. Also from I, cut eight lower leaf sections. From H, cut eight upper leaf sections. From B, cut four each petal sections and flower centers. From D, cut four flower cups.

Pin appliqués to background as follows: vine 5" from one short end (top) and centered between sides; place flowers around vine at 12, 3, 6, and 9 o'clock positions. Place a pair of leaves in between, one inside vine, the other outside. Fuse and stitch, using peach thread for edges of all flower parts, teal for edges of all exposed vine and leaf parts.

Assembly: Pin background to backing and center on a same-size piece of batting. Stitch a ½" seam all around, leaving a 5" opening at top edge. Trim seams to ¼". Turn and close opening. Topstitch ¼" from edges all around. Fold up bottom edge 11½" to form pocket. Stitch sides along topstitching. Turn top edge 2" to wrong side to form casing; slip-stitch along top edge to secure. Insert dowel. Tie twine to ends of dowel to hang calendar holder. Insert calendar in pocket.

BUN WARMER

SIZE: 25" across.

ADDITIONAL MATERIALS: Fabrics: 1¼ yards D, small amounts of A, B, G, H, and I. Ecru cotton cording, 2½ yards.

DIRECTIONS: Enlarge quarter pattern for bun warmer on a 2" grid; complete pattern. Use to cut two from D, for background and backing, adding ¼" seam allowances. From B, cut four petal sections; from A, cut four cups; from G, cut four centers; from H cut eight upper leaf sections; from I cut eight lower leaf sections. Also from I, cut two ⅞" × 18" strips, for stems.

Press long edges of strips ¼" to wrong side. Pin in a crisscross centered over background. Over each end, pin a flower; 2¼" from each flower, pin a pair of leaves with tips pointing toward flower and stems inserted under strips. Appliqué centers and cups with peach thread, petals with blue-gray, leaves with teal. Also with teal, straight stitch along edges of strips.

Add cording and assemble following General Directions.

To assemble projects, place backgrounds on backing pieces, right sides facing and raw edges even. Place both on batting cut to same size. Stitch around, along basted line if edges are corded or making ¼" seams, unless otherwise indicated; leave an opening for turning. Clip curves and angles; turn to right side. Slip-stitch openings closed. Press lightly.

CALENDAR HOLDER

SIZE: 12¾" × 25¾", accommodating a 12" square calendar; adjust dimensions to fit calendars slightly smaller or larger.

ADDITIONAL MATERIALS: Fabrics: ⅞ yard E,

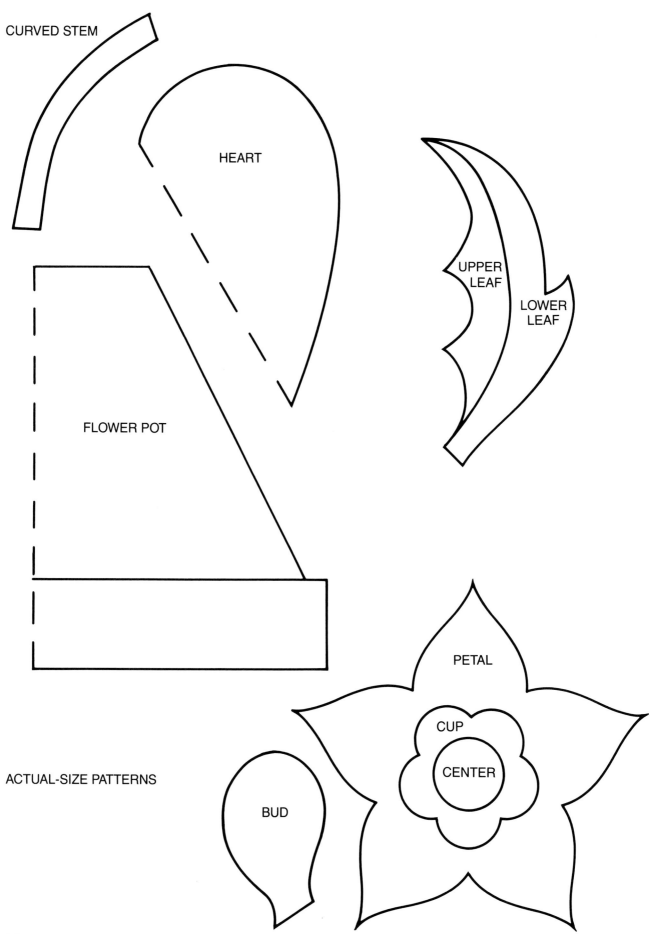

CURVED STEM

HEART

UPPER LEAF

LOWER LEAF

FLOWER POT

PETAL

CUP

CENTER

ACTUAL-SIZE PATTERNS

BUD

PATTERN FOR BUN WARMER

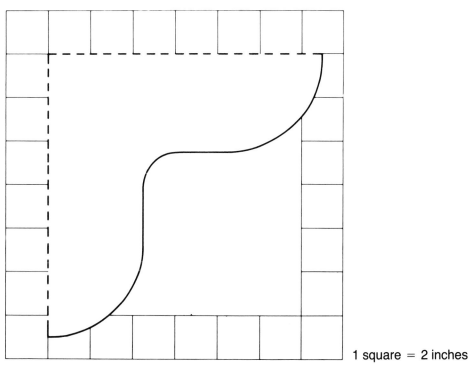

1 square = 2 inches

PLACE MAT

SIZE: 17″ × 14″.

ADDITIONAL MATERIALS: Fabrics (for each): ½ yard A, small amounts of B, C, D, F, G, and I; scraps of H.

DIRECTIONS: Be sure to add desired seam allowance to squares and rectangles before cutting. From A, cut a 14″ × 10″ rectangle for background. Make a 2″ square template for border patches. From B, cut two petal sections, one cup, and eight border patches. From C cut two flower centers and four border patches. From D cut one petal section, two cups, and eight border patches. From F cut one flower pot, using half pattern. From G cut two buds, one flower center, and eight border patches. From H cut four upper leaf sections. From I cut four lower leaf sections, two curved stems, and three ¼″ × 3¼″ strips for straight stems.

Center flower pot on background ½″ from bottom seam line. Referring to color photograph, arrange flowers, buds, and leaves. Fuse and stitch using closest matching thread color for each piece. Using same close zigzag stitch, machine-embroider a straight line across rim of flower pot, as indicated by fine line on pattern.

For side borders, arrange and stitch patches in the following vertical rows: G, D, B, D, G. Stitch to sides of background. For top and bottom borders, arrange and stitch patches in the following horizontal rows: B, G, C, D, B, D, C, G, B. Stitch across top and bottom of background.

Cut backing from A and batting to same size as place mat front. Assemble following General Directions.

BOOKMARKS

SIZE: Approximately 3½″.

ADDITIONAL MATERIALS: **For each:** Fabrics: scraps of C and G. Ecru cotton cording, ⅜ yard. Ecru grosgrain ribbon ⅜″ wide, ½ yard.

DIRECTIONS: From C, cut two petal sections (add ¼″ seam allowance), one flower center. From G, cut one flower cup, two hearts, using half heart pattern. Fuse and stitch flower center to cup and both to one petal section, using peach thread.

Place cording around appliquéd petal section or one heart. Pin ribbon end at top, even with fabric edges; roll up rest of ribbon and pin to center of fabric shape. Assemble with matching backing and batting, following General Directions and taking care not to catch ribbon roll in seam. Trim opposite ribbon end on an angle.

PILLOWS AND QUILTS: A WARM TRADITION

What could be lovelier than a choice selection of cozy bed quilts and plump pillows? Choose from a selection of favorite motifs to harmonize with your decorating scheme. The personal touches you add will help turn these quilt and pillow projects into treasured family heirlooms.

Pretty Pillows

Shadow quilting shows up especially well on pillows, which are always welcome gifts or accessories in one's home. These day lily and rosebud designs will give a touch of romance to country settings. A more tailored look can be achieved by finishing the edges without the ruffles.

SIZE: 12½" square, plus ruffle.

EQUIPMENT: Paper for patterns. Pencil. Ruler. Scissors. Dressmaker's tracing (carbon) paper. Dry ball-point pen. Embroidery hoop and needle. Sewing needle. Sewing machine. Steam iron.

MATERIALS: For each pillow: White cotton-blend fabric 36" wide, 1 yard. White voile 44" wide, ⅔ yard. Quilt batting, 18" square. DMC six-strand embroidery floss, one skein each: yellow #726, gold #729, light green #3348, medium green #906 for day lily; medium pink #957, deep pink #892, me-

ROSEBUD PILLOW

1—Bright pink #7603 (2)   3—Pale green #7907
2—Peach #7104 (2)   4—Grass green #7342 (2)

1 square = 1 inch

1 square = 1 inch

1—Bright yellow #7117 (4)
2—Pale green #7907
3—Grass green #7342 (2)

dium green #906 for rosebud. DMC Floralia three-ply Persian yarn, one skein of each color listed in color key unless otherwise indicated in parentheses. White sewing thread. Polyester fiberfill.

DIRECTIONS: For each: Cut white cotton-blend fabric into two 18″ squares for pillow front and lining, and one 13″ square for pillow back. Using ruler and pencil, draw lines across pattern, connecting grid lines. Enlarge pattern by copying on paper ruled in 1″ squares. Use dressmaker's carbon and dry ball-point pen to transfer design to center of one 18″ fabric square; include seam line (12½″ square around pattern). Place marked fabric in embroidery hoop. Referring to stitch detail on page 74 and pillow color key, fill in each numbered section on pattern with satin stitch; cut yarn into 36″ lengths and use all three plies together in needle. Stitch each section in a single direction; however, specific direction of stitches is not important. (**Note:** Do not embroider day lily stamens yet.)

When all satin stitch is complete, remove fabric from embroidery hoop; steam-press. Clip yarn ends close to back of fabric. Cut an 18″ square from voile. Place remaining 18″ white fabric square on work surface, face down. Place batting square, embroidered square (right side up), then voile square on white square with edges even. Place all layers in embroidery hoop, making sure all layers are smooth. Referring to page 74 for stitch details, work floss embroidery as follows: First, use four plies to backstitch outer circle, using gold #729 for day lily or deep pink #892 for rosebud. Next, use two plies to quilt around flowers and leaves with a small running (quilting) stitch: For day lily, use medium green #906 around leaves and stem, gold #729 around flower petals, light green #3348

around flower center sections; for rosebud, use medium green #906 around leaves, stems, and bud, and deep pink #892 around flower petals. For day lily only, embroider stamens: Bring floss up through all layers from back, then stitch stamens on voile only and bring floss back through all layers to end strand. Work stamen stems in stem stitch, using one ply of medium green #906; work stamen tips (ovals) in satin stitch, using three plies of yellow #726.

When center embroidery is complete, fill in background by placing a French knot at each dot on pattern. Use all six plies of floss in needle, twist floss only once around needle for each knot, and alternate medium green #906 French knots with yellow #726 (for day lily) or medium pink #957 (for rosebud) as shown in color photograph.

Remove pillow front from embroidery hoop. Baste through all layers near seam line, to keep edges of layers even. Measure and mark ½″ seam allowance outside marked seam line all around pillow front. Trim layers to this line.

From remaining voile, cut 6″-wide strips and piece together at short ends until strip is 3 yards long. Join strip ends to make a large ring. Fold ring in half lengthwise, right side out; press along fold. Work two rows of basting ¼″ and ½″ in from raw edge, sewing through both layers; pull threads to gather ring to 54″ around. Adjust gathers evenly and pin, then baste ruffle around pillow front, with raw edges even and with ruffle resting on pillow front. Sew ruffle in place, making ½″ seam. Place 13″-square pillow back on pillow front, right sides facing, edges even, and enclosing ruffle. Sew all around with ½″ seam, leaving a 6″ opening for turning. Turn right side out, stuff with fiberfill to desired firmness. Turn raw edges in and slip-stitch opening closed.

Red and White Pattern Play

The Wild Goose Chase quilt pattern with its scalloped borders shown here is more than one hundred years old. Each of its basic blocks has a blue triangle in one corner. When its thirty-six blocks are rotated into position, nine pinwheels are formed. The star-pattern pillows shown in Ohio Star, Pinwheel Star, Compass, and Radiant Star designs offer challenges to the quilter.

MATERIALS FOR PILLOWS: Cotton fabrics: White, white background with tiny red print (white print), plus five coordinating red calicoes—red tiny floral (red #1), red small floral (red #2), red floral and pindots (red #3), red geometric (red #4), red large floral (red #5); see Materials in individual directions for amounts. White sewing and quilting thread. Muslin for backing/lining, 16″ square for each. Batting. Cotton cording, ¼″, 1⅝ yards for each smaller pillow, 2 yards for each larger pillow. Polyester fiberfill.

GENERAL DIRECTIONS FOR PILLOWS: Review "Quilting Compendium," pages 69–76. Make templates for patches as needed: Trace actual-size template patterns as given on pages 36 and 38. For all other templates, draw squares and rectangles using measurements given. Unless otherwise indicated, triangles are squares cut diagonally in half. Add seam allowance when cutting.

A—6″ triangle	**H**—1⅞″ square
B—See pattern	**I**—2⅜″ triangle
C—See pattern	**J**—2⅜″ square
D—See pattern	**K**—2″ triangle
E—See pattern	**L**—See pattern
F—2⅞″ square	**M**—See pattern
G—2⅞″ triangle	**N**—See pattern

Make templates and cut out patches as indicated in individual directions. Arrange patches following piecing diagram. Stitch together those patches as shown in areas within heavy outlines to form units, then join units and make borders as indicated.

Quilting: Layer batting and patchwork on top of muslin square. Quilt around each patch, ⅛″ inside seams.

Assembly: Cut backing from largest amount of fabric to match size of pillow front. **Cording:** Cut remaining backing fabric into 1″-wide strips on the bias. Piece together to measure 2″ more than perimeter of pillow. Place cotton cording on wrong side of strip, lengthwise down center. Bring long edges together and stitch ¼″ from edges, using zipper foot of sewing machine to get close to cording. Pin cording around pillow front, raw edges even and ends overlapping slightly so that cut ends "disappear" into seam allowance; machine-baste as close as possible to cording.

Place pillow front on backing. Sew around on top of basting stitches, leaving an opening at center of one side. Clip corners and turn to right side. Stuff with fiberfill or pillow form, then slip-stitch opening closed.

PINWHEEL STAR (front row, left)

SIZE: 14″ square.

MATERIALS: ½ yard red #4, ⅛ yard each white, white print, and red #1.

DIRECTIONS: Note: D and E templates are not symmetrical; use match marks to avoid confusion. From white fabric, cut four D; reverse template and cut the same from red #4. From white print, cut four E and four K. Cut the same pieces from red #1, reversing E template.

As shown in heavily outlined area on piecing diagram, join K patch to E, then join E to D to form one triangular unit. Create seven other units referring to piecing diagram for fabrics; stitch units together in pairs along E and K sides to form larger triangle. Longest edge of large triangle should measure 10½″ inside seam allowances.

For borders, cut four 1¾″ × 14″ (add desired seam allowance) strips from white print. Center one strip along longest edge of each large triangle. Stitch large triangles together in pairs along D and K edges, then pairs together to form square pillow top, continuing straight seams to miter borders.

PINWHEEL COMPASS (front row, right)

SIZE: 14″ square.

MATERIALS: ½ yard white print, ⅛ yard each white, red #4, and red #5.

DIRECTIONS: Patchwork pattern is identical to Pinwheel Star, but fabrics are used differently. From red #5, cut four D. Reverse template and cut the same from white print. From red #5, cut four each E and K; cut the same from white, reversing template E.

Arrange as shown in piecing diagram, and follow directions for piecing Pinwheel Star, but cut borders from red #4.

OHIO STAR WITH PINWHEEL CENTER (back row, right)

SIZE: 15½″ square.

MATERIALS: ½ yard red #4, ¼ yard each white and white print, scraps of red #2.

DIRECTIONS: From white, cut four each C, F, and M. From white print, cut four G. From red #2, cut four M. From red #4, cut eight G.

Arrange patches as shown in piecing diagram. First join patches to form square unit heavily outlined; repeat for three more square units. Join square units to form center square. Create four rectangular units as heavily outlined. Join two to opposite sides of center square. Sew F patches to sides of two remaining rectangular units. Refer to diagram and join to form center block, which should measure 11½″ inside seam allowances. From white print, cut four border rectangles 1⅞″ × 11½″; from red #2 cut four corner patches 1⅞″ square (H). Stitch two border strips to opposite sides of block. Stitch an H patch to ends of remaining border strips, then sew to top and bottom of block.

OHIO STAR WITH TRIANGLE BORDER (back row, left)

SIZE: 15½″ square.

MATERIALS: ½ yard white print, ¼ yard white and red #5, ⅛ yard red #3.

DIRECTIONS: From white, cut four G, sixteen N. From white print, cut four each C and F. From red #3, cut eight G. From red #5, cut one B, twelve N.

Stitch a white G to each side of B to form center square. Using this center square and colors as shown in piecing diagram, assemble block same as for Ohio Star with Pinwheel Center. For each border strip, first join nonmatching N patches to form parallelograms as shown on piecing diagram, then stitch these together in a row, adding a white N at the end. Stitch a border strip to each side of block, then stitch ends of border strips together at corners.

PINWHEEL STAR

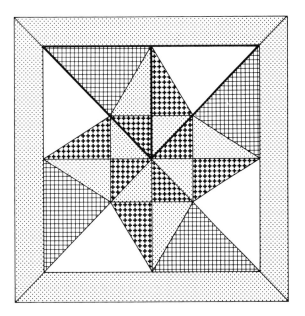

□	White
▒	White print
▦	Red #4
▨	Red #1

OHIO STAR WITH PINWHEEL CENTER

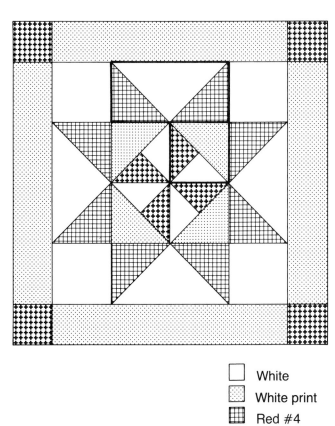

□	White
▒	White print
▦	Red #4
▨	Red #2

PIECING DIAGRAMS

PINWHEEL COMPASS

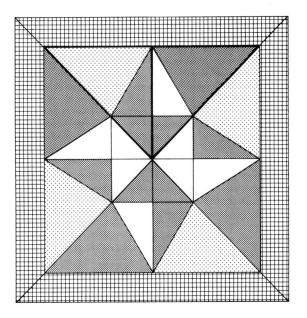

□	White
▒	White print
▦	Red #4
▓	Red #5

OHIO STAR WITH TRIANGLE BORDER

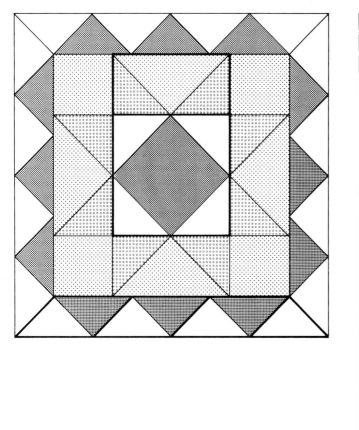

White
White print
Red #3
Red #5

RADIANT STAR

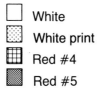

White
White print
Red #4
Red #5

RADIANT STAR (back row, center)

SIZE: 15½" square.

MATERIALS: ½ yard red #5, ¼ yard each white print and red #4, ⅛ yard white.

DIRECTIONS: From white, cut four each I and J. From both white print and red #5, cut four K and eight L. From red #4, cut four A.

Assemble L patches in unmatched pairs to form diamonds. Join diamonds in pairs to form a quarter star unit, as heavily outlined in the piecing diagram. Join quarters to form half stars, then join halves for completed star. Fit white patches between star points to complete center square. Stitch an A patch to each side of square; resulting block should measure 11½" square inside seam allowances. For borders, cut, adding seam allowance, four 2" × 11½" rectangles from white print. Stitch two to opposite sides of block. Join unmatched K patches together along their long edges to form corner squares. Stitch a corner square to each end of remaining border as shown on piecing diagram, then stitch to top and bottom of block.

ACTUAL-SIZE PATTERNS FOR PILLOWS

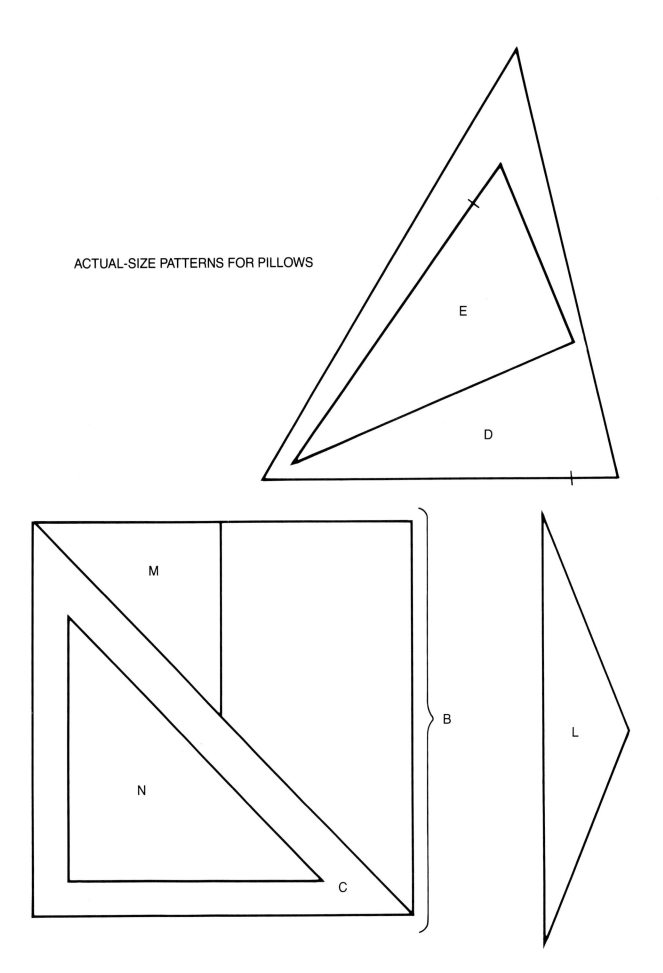

WILD GOOSE CHASE QUILT

SIZE: Approximately 67″ square.

MATERIALS: Fabrics 44″ wide: red print (for backing and binding), 3¾ yards; white, 4½ yards; blue pin dot, 3 yards; ⅜ yard each pink calico and red. White and red sewing thread. White quilting thread. Batting.

DIRECTIONS: Review "Quilting Compendium," pages 69–76. Quilt is made up of thirty-six quilt blocks in six rows of six, surrounded by a pieced and then a scalloped border with a quilted design. Trace and make templates for triangles A and B, shown here actual size on page 38. Mark and cut the following from fabrics:

From white, 972 A
From blue, 756 A
From red, 72B
From pink, 72B

Quilt block (make thirty-six): Stitch twenty each white and blue A patches together along their longest edges to form small squares. Join all squares in pairs with white edges together, forming a center triangle. Stitch two pairs together to form a square unit with center triangles stacked vertically (see piecing diagram). Square unit should measure 3¼″ inside seam allowances. Stitch six white A's together in pairs along one short side to form triangular corner units. Stitch remaining white and blue A together in same manner. Arrange square units, red and pink B triangles, and triangular units together following piecing diagram. The extending dash lines mark diagonal rows. Piece patches together in each row, then stitch Row 1 to Row 2, Row 2 to Row 3, Row 4 to Row 5, and Row 3 to Row 5, matching seams carefully. Resulting block should measure 9″ square inside seam allowances.

Quilt top: Arrange blocks into six horizontal rows of six blocks. Referring to color photograph, turn

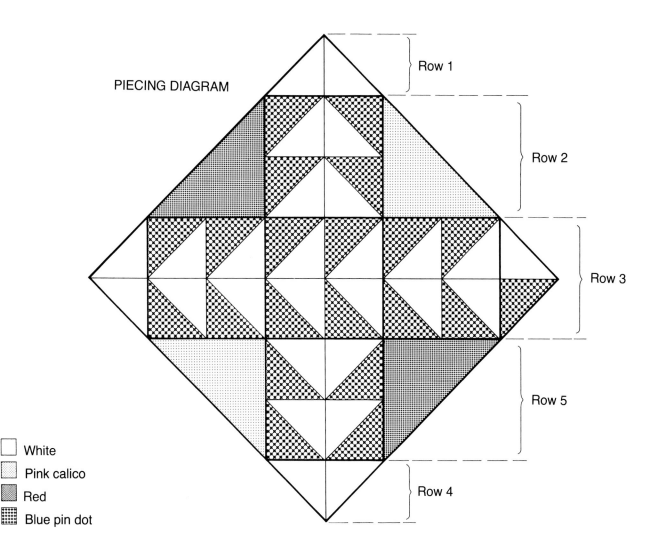

PIECING DIAGRAM

Row 1

Row 2

Row 3

Row 5

Row 4

☐ White

▦ Pink calico

▨ Red

▦ Blue pin dot

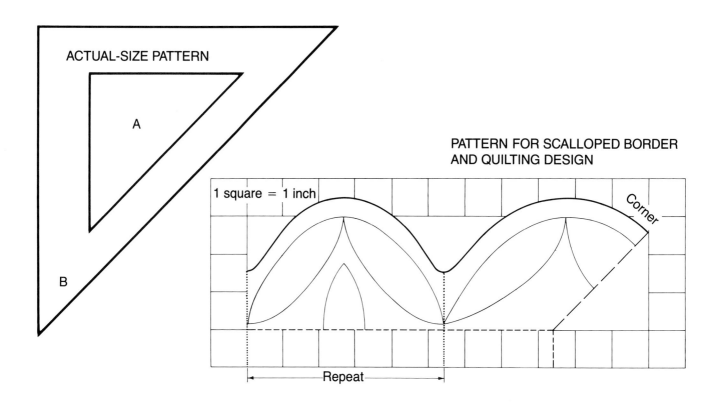

ACTUAL-SIZE PATTERN

A

B

PATTERN FOR SCALLOPED BORDER
AND QUILTING DESIGN

1 square = 1 inch

Corner

Repeat

blocks so that red and pink triangles alternate across top of rows and blue and white corner triangles come together, forming pinwheels. There will be nine pinwheels altogether. Carefully matching seams, sew blocks into rows, then sew rows together.

Pieced Border: Make template for patches: Mark and cut a 3″ square diagonally in half to form triangle. Use template to cut

   76 triangles from white
   38 from blue
   20 from red
   18 from pink

Stitch a white triangle to each red, blue, and pink triangle along their long edges to form a square. For side borders, arrange squares in a vertical row with white patches toward the inside; begin with a square containing a red triangle on top, place a square with a blue triangle underneath, then one with a pink triangle, then one with a blue triangle. Repeat color sequence for a total of eighteen squares. Stitch white edges to sides of quilt top, matching seams between quilt blocks with every third square. Work top and bottom borders same as for sides, but use twenty squares horizontally; work sequence of colors right to left along top, left to right along bottom. Quilt top should now measure 60″ square inside seam allowances.

Scalloped Border: From white, cut four 4″ × 68½″ rectangles (add seam allowance). Pin one to each

outside edge of pieced border, with excess fabric extending equally at either side. Stitch, mitering corners. Enlarge pattern for scalloped border and markings. Place pattern for scalloped border with long dash line matching mitered corner seam and short dash line on seam between scalloped border and pieced border. Using dressmaker's carbon paper and dry ball-point pen, transfer heavy curvy outline (indicating cutting line) and fine lines (indicating quilting lines). Reverse pattern to turn corner, match up dash lines, and transfer rest of corner, then repeat the scallop section between dotted lines all the way across side until you reach corner square of pieced border. Transfer corner. Continue in this manner until quilting design is marked all around. Do not cut out.

Quilting: Piece backing and cut batting to slightly larger than quilt top; assemble layers. Quilt as follows: Quilt all patches ⅛″ inside seams. Quilt ⅛″ beyond seam between borders. Quilt scalloped border along marked lines.

Binding: Stitch ⅛″ inside heavy outline of scalloped border, through all layers. Cut along outline through all layers. From remainder of red print fabric, cut 1¼″-wide strips on the bias (measurement includes seam allowances). Join to form one long strip. Press one long edge ¼″ to wrong side. Pin-baste opposite long edge to front of quilt along scalloped edge, easing it around curves. Stitch ¼″ from raw edges. Turn strip to backing; pin. Slipstitch along pressed edge.

Autumn Leaves

This Oak Leaf quilt, in a palette of autumn colors, offers beauty and warmth for the master bedroom. This quilt is framed with a wide contrasting border in a solid color.

SIZE: 92" × 109½".

EQUIPMENT: Pencil. Ruler. Paper and tracing paper for patterns. Dressmaker's tracing (carbon) paper. Dry ball-point pen. Tailor's chalk. Straight pins. Sewing and quilting needles. Quilting frame.

MATERIALS: Unbleached muslin 38"/39" wide, 5 yards. Closely woven cotton fabrics 44" wide; orange, 3¼ yards; gold, 5¼ yards; brown print, 2¼ yards; rust print, 2¼ yards; green print, 3 yards. Fabric for lining 38"/39" wide (such as muslin), 8 yards. Sewing thread to match fabrics. White quilting thread. Batting.

DIRECTIONS: Using pencil and ruler, draw lines across patterns for border section and quilt block, connecting grid lines. Enlarge patterns by copying on paper ruled in 1" squares. Solid lines indicate appliqués, dotted lines quilting. Make tracing of quilt block, then complete quarter pattern as follows: Cut 17½" square of paper and place flat. Position tracing on top, so that edges indicated by outer solid lines are even with one corner of paper; place carbon paper between and trace design lines to transfer pattern to paper. Rotate pattern clockwise 90°; align pattern with corner of paper and edge of transferred design; trace. Turn and trace pattern twice more to complete pattern. Use border and quilt block patterns to make separate patterns for pieces A, B, C, D, E, F, and G.

Quilt Blocks: From muslin, cut twenty pieces 18" square for quilt blocks. On right side, center quilt

1 square = 1 inch

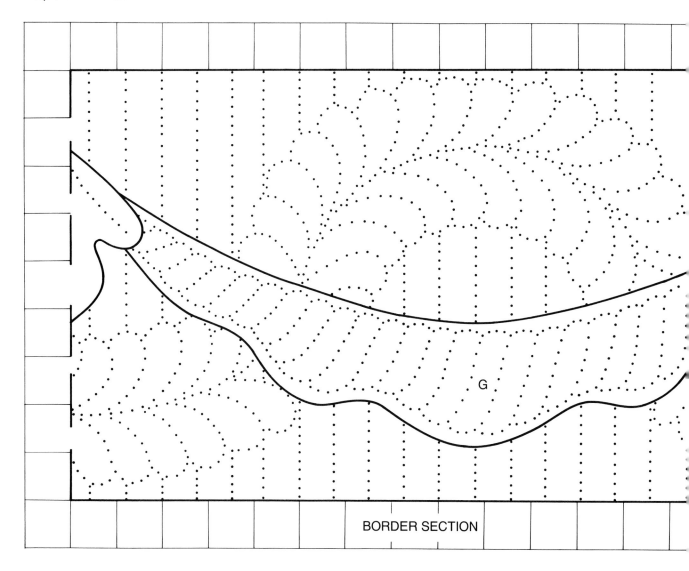

BORDER SECTION

block pattern over each block and transfer main outline, using dressmaker's tracing (carbon) paper and dry ball-point pen; there will be ¼" muslin all around pattern. See "How to Appliqué," page 75. Using patterns, cut and prepare the following pieces for hand appliqué as directed:

    50 A's (10 from brown fabric, 10 from rust, 15 from orange, 15 from gold)
    20 B's from green
    20 C's (10 from orange, 10 from gold)
    160 D's (80 from brown, 80 from rust)
    80 E's (40 from brown, 40 from rust)

Cut orange, gold, and green pieces along length of goods close to one selvage, rather than across, leaving the opposite side intact for cutting borders and strips later.

Blocks are appliquéd using two color schemes. Referring to color illustration, appliqué ten blocks as follows: Begin by appliquéing a brown A to center of a green B piece; appliqué B pieces to center of gold C piece, following pattern for placement. Appliqué the C piece with eight brown D pieces to block. To diagonally opposite corners, appliqué two brown E's; appliqué two rust E's to remaining corners. Do not appliqué corner A pieces at this time. In same manner, appliqué remaining ten blocks, using rust A and D pieces and orange C's.

Lay out blocks into five horizontal rows of four blocks each, alternating color schemes throughout and matching E pieces of the same color where corners meet. With right sides facing and edges even and making ¼" seams, stitch quilt blocks into

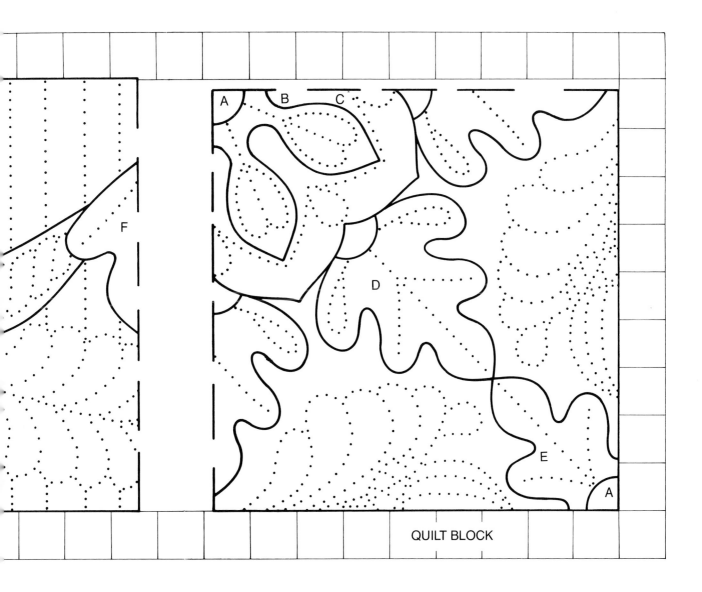

QUILT BLOCK

rows; stitch rows together. To center of each group of four E pieces, appliqué an A piece (orange to rust, gold to brown). Along sides, trim A's and use only half piece, plus seam allowance; use quarter pieces at corners, plus seam allowance. Quilt top should measure 70½" × 88".

Border strips: From reserved green fabric, cut two 1¾" × 73" and two 1¾" × 90½" strips. Stitch short strips to short sides of quilt top and long strips to long sides, centering strips and making ¼" seams. Pin raw edges of strip ends together. Beginning at each corner of quilt top, stitch a seam at a 45° angle across ends, mitering corner; trim seam allowance. From reserved orange fabric, cut two 10" × 92" and two 10" × 109½" strips. Stitch strips in place as be-

fore, allowing 9¾" to extend beyond sides at each corner; miter corners and trim seam allowance as for green strip. Quilt top should measure 92" × 109½".

Find center block along one long side. Using tailor's chalk and ruler, draw lines extending from seams across borders, 17½" apart. Repeat marks all around border. Beginning at center of one long side, place pattern for border section between marks, so that dash lines on pattern align with marks. Transfer appliqué outlines to fabric, using dressmaker's carbon and dry ball-point pen. Move pattern to right or left and align at next set of marks. Continue to transfer pattern to border all around, working outward from center on each side; transfer only partial pattern at corners, ending at seam as shown in illustration. Using patterns, cut

22 F pieces from brown print fabric

18 G pieces from gold

Prepare for hand appliqué as directed. Using tracing paper and pencil, trace marked lines of truncated G's at corners; use tracing to cut four appliqués from gold fabric. Appliqué G's to orange border along marked lines, then appliqué F pieces to G joinings as shown on pattern.

Quilting: Using dressmaker's carbon and dry ball-point pen, transfer quilting lines from quilt block and border patterns to quilt top. Using tailor's chalk and ruler, draw quilting lines on green border strip as follows: Beginning at one corner, draw a diagonal line parallel to and ¾" from corner seam. Continue to draw parallel lines ¾" apart around border; lines will cross seams at two opposite corners.

To make lining, cut two pieces 37" × 92" and one piece 37½" × 92"; sew together on long edges with ½" seams, to make piece 92" × 109½". Cut batting same size. Place lining flat, wrong side up. Place batting on top and anchor with two long stitches crossing in center. Place marked quilt top over batting, right side up. Pin layers together to hold, then baste generously lengthwise, crosswise, and diagonally.

Using white quilting thread, quilt on all marked lines, starting at center of quilt and working around and outward. Also, quilt just outside each appliqué, close to seam. See detail on page 76 for quilting stitch.

Edging: From gold fabric, cut strip 2½" wide and 11¼ yards long, piecing to get length. Pin strip around front of quilt, right sides facing and matching raw edges. Stitch through all layers with ¾" seam, turning in end of strip ¼". Turn strip to lining side, fold in edge ¼", and slip-stitch in place.

Appliqué Pussycat

Cat lovers of all ages will delight in this colorful kittenish quilt that includes whimsical appliqués in bird, mouse, and fish motifs. The quilt is sized for a single bed, but may be expanded to fit a larger one, or reduced to fit a crib or cot.

SIZE 55½" × 83¼".

MATERIALS: Muslin 44" wide, 6¼ yards (includes lining). Closely woven cotton fabric 44" wide: 2⅜ yards black; ⅜ yard each brown and rust; ½ yard each beige and gold; ¼ yard tan, dark gray and dark green; ⅛ yard each medium gray, light gray, medium gray-green, pale gray-green, olive green, and aqua. Thin batting. Matching sewing threads.

DIRECTIONS: Review "Quilting Compendium," pages 69–76. From muslin, cut piece 28½" × 170" and set aside for lining. From remaining muslin, cut the following background pieces, referring to numbers on quilt diagram: two pieces 10¾" × 15½" (#1 and #3), one piece 21¼" × 15½" (#2), 8½" × 44" (#4), 16" × 44" (#5), 6" × 44" (#6), 14" × 16½" (#7), 14" × 10¾" (#8), 14" × 15½" (#9), 5½" × 44" (#10), 12¼" × 44" (#11); two pieces 4¼" × 82" (#12 and #13). From black fabric, cut strips 1⅝" wide for

43

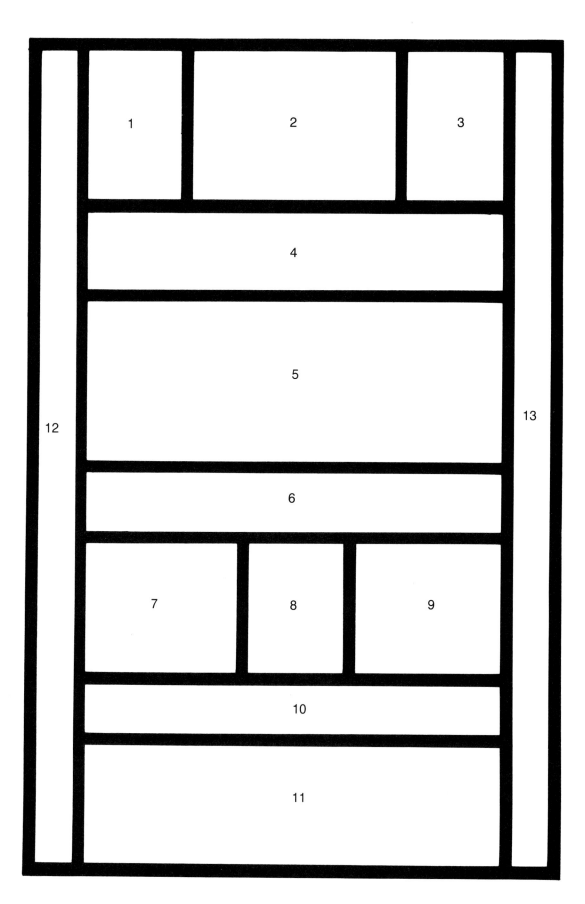

sashing: four 82″ long, six 44″ long, two 15½″ long, and two 14″ long. Also from black, cut four 2¾″-wide border strips, two 56½″ long and two 84″ long.

Appliqués: Enlarge appliqué patterns as directed (each pattern number corresponds to a background number). Referring to color illustration, cut appliqués from fabric for each cat and prepare for hand appliqué. Cut five birds, all with black legs: Cut four of 4A, two with brown upper bodies and rust breasts, one with an all-rust body (omitting breast), and one with an all-dark gray body; cut one of 4B with a light gray body. For background piece #5, cut eight each of 5A from dark green, 5B from medium gray-green, and 5C from olive green, reversing pattern for four of each. Cut nine of 5D from aqua, reversing for four. Cut five mice from the three fabrics as desired, substituting a curved tail for two mice. Cut eight fish from aqua, pale gray-green, medium gray-green, olive green, dark green, and pale gray (cut six of 10A, reversing for one; cut two of 10B).

Arrange prepared appliqués on background pieces as shown, allowing at least ⅜″ margin all around on tight-fitting pieces. Pin, baste, and slip-stitch appliqués in place, using matching thread.

Assembling: Arrange background pieces 1, 2, and 3 in a horizontal row, with 15½″ black strips between pieces. Join pieces and strips with ¼″ seams. Re-peat with pieces 7, 8, and 9, using 14″ strips. Arrange pieces 1 through 11 vertically as shown in quilt diagram with 44″ strips between rows; join as before. Piece should measure 44″ × 81½″. Trim ends of 1⅝″-wide black strips to match length and attach to sides. Trim muslin pieces 12 and 13 to match length and attach. Quilt top should measure 53¾″ × 81½″.

Quilting: From reserved muslin, cut two pieces 28¼″ × 83¼″. Sew pieces together on long edges with ½″ seams, to make lining 55½″ × 83¼″. Cut batting same size. Layer the three pieces, centering quilt top on batting, and pin. Baste through layers lengthwise, crosswise, and diagonally in both directions. Topstitch along each seam joining black and muslin pieces; use black or white thread in needle, depending upon position of stitching (use white thread in bobbin).

Binding Edges: On each border strip, press under one long edge ¼″. With quilt right side up, place a longer strip along each side, right sides of fabric facing and matching raw edges; trim ends of strips to match top and bottom of quilt. Stitch strips in place with ¼″ seams. Turn strips to wrong side and slip-stitch folded edges to lining. Repeat at top and bottom with shorter strips, but do not trim ends; turn in excess fabric at each end and slip-stitch closed.

JUNIOR ATTRACTIONS

One of the loveliest things about quilts and quilted accessories is how soft and cuddly they are. Because they have no sharp corners or hard surfaces, they're ideal for the nursery and preschoolers. The projects in this group are not only practical, they're also decorative and fun. Here are eye-catching quilted toys, building blocks, wall hangings . . . and more.

Nursery Pals

Pussycat, pussycat, where are you? Here in the nursery, charming baby with a quilt and all sorts of practical matching accessories (pillow, bibs, diaper holder, towels, wall organizer, and what you will) to make baby's care as easy as can be.

SIZES: Quilt, 30″ × 45″; pillow, 12″ × 13″.

EQUIPMENT: Pencil. Ruler. Paper for patterns. Straight pins. Scissors. Dressmaker's tracing (carbon) paper. Dry ball-point pen. Sewing and embroidery needles. Sewing machine (optional). Yardstick. Tailor's chalk or water-erasable marking pen.

MATERIALS: **For quilt:** Closely woven cotton fabric 45″ wide: pale pink, 1½ yards; aqua, 1 yard. Batting, 30″ × 45″. **For pillow:** Polyester fiberfill. **For each:** Closely woven cotton fabric: white, 45″ wide, ½ yard; scraps of pink calico, pink dotted, and medium blue. Sewing threads to match fabrics. Six-strand embroidery floss, one skein each of rose and pale blue.

QUILT

DIRECTIONS: From aqua fabric, cut 30″ × 45″ piece for front of quilt. From pale pink fabric, cut 36″ × 51″ piece for backing and border.

Appliqué: Draw lines across pattern for Kitten Quilt, connecting grid lines. Enlarge patterns by copying on paper ruled in 1″ squares. Read "How to Appliqué" on page 75. Following directions, mark pieces as follows: head, body, and feet on white fabric (transferring fine embroidery lines to face); tail and stripes on pink calico; heart and ears on pink dotted; pupils on medium blue. Cut out pieces as directed and prepare for hand appliqué. Appliqué body to quilt front, centered between long sides and 14″ from bottom edge. Appliqué remaining pieces where indicated on pattern. Embroider face, using two strands of floss in needle: With blue, work pupils in straight stitch and eyes and whiskers in outline stitch; with rose, work nose in satin stitch and mouth in outline stitch.

Assembly: Place pale pink backing piece right side down on work surface. Center batting and appliquéd front on backing, right side up and with edges even. Baste through all layers lengthwise, crosswise, and diagonally in both directions. Using yardstick and tailor's chalk or water-erasable marking pen, lightly mark diagonal lines 10″ apart across quilt front in both directions, skipping over cat, for a large diamond pattern. Quilt by hand around each appliqué piece and embroidered detail, then quilt along diagonal lines, working outward from center. When all quilting is complete, fold each edge of backing 1″ to wrong side; press. Fold backing over edges of quilt and slip-stitch folded edges to quilt front, mitering corners. Remove basting threads.

PILLOW

DIRECTIONS: Read appliqué directions above for quilt. Enlarge pattern for Kitten Pillow as directed for quilt appliqués. Mark two cat bodies on wrong side of white fabric; cut out ¼″ beyond marked lines. On right side of one body (front), transfer embroidery lines to face. Cut body pieces and appliqué to front as for quilt; embroider in same manner.

Assembly: Place appliquéd and plain cat bodies together with right sides facing and edges even. Sew around sides and head, making ¼″ seam and leaving bottom open. Pin base into opening at bottom with right sides facing and edges even. Sew all around, making ¼″ seam and leaving an opening for turning. Turn cat right side out; stuff firmly. Fold raw edges ¼″ to inside and slip-stitch opening closed.

LITTLE KITTEN BABY ACCESSORIES

EQUIPMENT: Ruler. Pencil. Paper for patterns. Dressmaker's tracing (carbon) paper. Dry ball-point pen. Straight pins. Scissors. Sewing machine with zigzag stitch. Sewing needle. Steam iron.

MATERIALS: Closely woven cotton fabric 45″ wide (see individual directions for colors and amounts). Sewing thread: white, pink, rose, aqua, deep blue. See individual directions for additional materials.

GENERAL DIRECTIONS: Using ruler and pencil, draw lines across pattern on next page, connecting grid lines. Enlarge patterns by copying on paper ruled in 1″ squares; complete half patterns, indicated by dash lines. (Fine lines on patterns indicate machine embroidery; heavy lines are pattern outlines.) Review "Quilting Compendium," pages 69–76. Following directions, transfer patterns and embroidery lines to fabric; cut out pieces. Position appliqué pieces on background fabric, following patterns for placement. Machine-appliqué pieces, using matching sewing thread. To embroider faces, use same stitch as for machine appliqué and work aqua eyes and whiskers, rose nose and mouth; fill in nose triangle with a wider column of machine stitching. Complete projects as directed below.

QUILT AND PILLOW PATTERNS

1 square = 1 inch

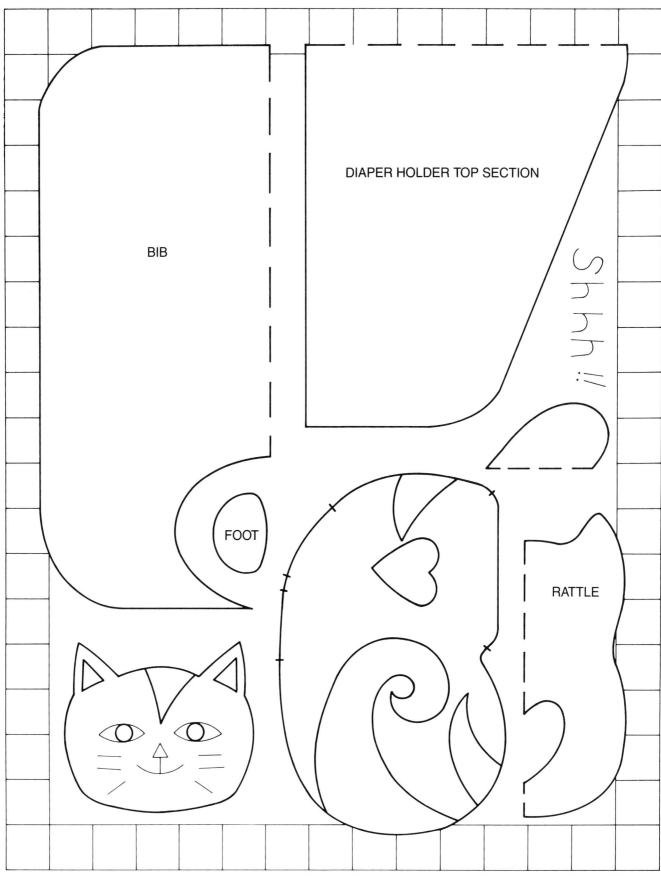

DIAPER HOLDER TOP SECTION

BIB

Shhh!!

FOOT

RATTLE

ACCESSORIES PATTERN

1 square = 1 inch

WASHCLOTH

ADDITIONAL MATERIALS: Pink washcloth. Scraps of pink calico and solid pink fabric.

DIRECTIONS: Read General Directions for Little Kitten Baby Accessories. Cut one larger heart from pink calico and one smaller heart from solid pink. Machine-appliqué calico heart to a corner of washcloth, 1¼" from edges. Appliqué solid pink heart to center of calico heart.

HAND TOWEL

ADDITIONAL MATERIALS: Pink hand towel. Scraps of white, pink, calico, and deep blue fabric.

DIRECTIONS: Read General Directions for Little Kitten Baby Accessories. Cut head from white fabric, ears and stripe from pink calico, and pupils from blue. Machine-appliqué head, centered, on front of towel, 4" above bottom short edge. Appliqué ears, stripe, and eyes on head. Machine-embroider face as directed above.

BATH TOWEL

ADDITIONAL MATERIALS: Pink bath towel. Large scrap of white fabric; scraps of pink calico, solid pink, and deep blue fabric.

DIRECTIONS: Read General Directions for Little Kitten Baby Accessories. Cut head, body, and feet from white fabric; tail, ears, and stripes from pink calico; one small heart from solid pink; and eyes from blue.

Machine-appliqué body, centered, on towel, 4¾" above bottom edge. Appliqué head and feet to towel, then remaining pieces to head and body. Machine-embroider face as directed above; machine-embroider outlines of feet with white thread.

DOOR SIGN

SIZE: 8¾" × 9".

ADDITIONAL MATERIALS: Large scraps of white, light blue, and blue gingham fabric; scraps of pink calico and solid pink fabric. Batting. Pink picot-edge ribbon ⅜" wide, 21".

DIRECTIONS: Read General Directions for Little Kitten Baby Accessories. Cut one piece 9¼" × 9½" each from solid blue and gingham fabric and bat-ting. Cut appliqués for cat and appliqué to center of solid blue rectangle (sign front) as for bath towel, omitting blue pupils and outer eyes. For eyes, draw a slightly curved line connecting inner and outer corners of each eye on pattern, for closed eyes. Transfer Shhh!! to upper right quarter of solid blue rectangle, using dressmaker's carbon and dry ball-point pen, as shown in color photograph. Machine-appliqué and embroider sign front as for bath towel, embroidering closed eyes with aqua and Shhh!! with rose; widen stitch from bottom to top of each exclamation mark.

When sign front is complete, place gingham rec-tangle on front piece, right sides facing and edges even. Place batting rectangle on wrong side of ging-ham. Sew layers together all around, rounding cor-ners and leaving an opening for turning at bottom edge. Trim batting close to seam. Turn sign right side out, fold raw edges in, and slip-stitch opening closed.

Cut a 12" length of ribbon. Fold ends ¼" to back, then pin to back of sign, 2" down from top edge and 1¼" in from each side edge, so ribbon forms an inverted V in center. Slip-stitch ribbon to back of sign on long edges and ends. Tie remaining ribbon in a bow; tack to center front of first ribbon strip at point of inverted V.

BIB

SIZE: 10¼" × 12¼".

ADDITIONAL MATERIALS: Pink calico fabric, 13" × 22"; scraps of white, solid pink, and deep blue fabric. Batting. Light blue single-fold bias tape ⅜" wide, 40".

DIRECTIONS: Read General Directions for Little Kitten Baby Accessories. Cut two bibs from pink calico and one bib from batting; cut head from white fabric, ears and stripe from solid pink, and pupils from blue. Machine-appliqué head, cen-tered, to one calico bib (front), 1¾" above bottom edge. Appliqué remaining pieces and embroider as for hand towel. Place plain calico bib (back) on bib front with right sides facing and edges even; place batting bib on wrong side of bib back. Sew layers together, making ¼" seam and leaving curved top edge open. Trim batting close to seam. Turn bib right side out. Pin bias tape around curved top edge on bib front with right sides facing, raw edges even, and equal lengths of tape extending from bib, for ties. Sew tape to bib, then fold tape over raw bib edges and slip-stitch folded edge of tape to back. Fold tie ends ¼" to inside, then slip-stitch long open edge of each tie.

QUIET RATTLE

SIZE: 3¾" × 6½".

ADDITIONAL MATERIALS: Large scrap pink calico fabric; scraps of white, deep blue, and solid pink fabric. Polyester fiberfill.

DIRECTIONS: Read General Directions for Little Kitten Baby Accessories. Cut two rattles from pink calico; cut appliqué pieces as for bib. Appliqué and embroider head on one rattle piece as for bib, matching raw edges of rattle and head. Place rattle shapes together with right sides facing and edges even. Sew outer edges together, making ¼" seam and leaving an opening at bottom for turning. Turn rattle right side out; stuff head firmly. Pin inner heart edges together with wrong sides facing; zigzag-stitch closed. Stuff bottom of rattle firmly, then fold raw edges in and slip-stitch opening closed.

DIAPER HOLDER

SIZE: 17" × 27¼", plus hook.

ADDITIONAL MATERIALS: Blue gingham, 1 yard. Light blue fabric, ½ yard. Scraps of white, solid pink, pink calico, and deep blue fabric. Plastic clothes hanger 17" wide. Heavy cardboard, 8" × 13". Batting.

DIRECTIONS: Read General Directions for Little Kitten Baby Accessories. From blue gingham, cut 21" × 45" side piece and 9" × 13½" base. Using patterns, cut four tops from light blue fabric and two from batting; two smaller hearts from solid pink; two larger hearts, two ears, and one forehead stripe from pink calico; one white head; and two deep blue eyes. Appliqué and embroider head as for hand towel, with head centered on one light blue top piece 2½" below point at top. Appliqué a calico heart 1" from each side of head, so that bottom of each heart is even with bottom of head. Appliqué a solid pink heart in center of each calico heart.

To assemble one top section, place a plain piece right side down on work surface. Place a batting piece on first piece, then appliquéd piece right side up on batting. Baste layers together along top and side edges. Assemble a second section with remaining top pieces. Place sections together with appliquéd top facing a plain top. Sew all six layers together, making two ¼" seams; begin ⅝" from top center and sew to bottom of side edge on each side. Turn layers right side out so appliquéd piece is on top. Fold in raw edges ¼" at top center and sew each

pair of fabric tops closed, leaving a 1¼" opening at center top.

Fold each short edge of gingham side piece ⅛", then again ⅝" to wrong side; topstitch, for hems. Pin one long edge of side piece all around gingham base piece with right sides facing and edges even, beginning ⅛" from center of one long side; there will be a ¼" gap between hemmed side edges. Sew side to base, making ¼" seam. Baste along remaining long edge of side piece. Gather edge to fit inside bottom edge of top section. Pin gathered edge to outer edges of top section, beginning and ending at center front, with right sides facing and edges even. Sew gathered edge to top section, making ¼" seam. Fold inner edges of top section ¼" to inside; slip-stitch to back of gathered edge. Remove any visible basting threads. Insert hook of hanger through opening at top of top section; place cardboard base on fabric base, inside completed diaper holder.

WALL ORGANIZER

SIZE: 15" × 21".

ADDITIONAL MATERIALS: Light blue fabric, ½ yard. Blue gingham, ¼ yard. Scraps of white, solid pink, pink calico, and deep blue fabric. Batting. Thin wooden strip ½" wide, 14". Flat elastic ⅜" wide, 30". Two plastic rings, 1" diameter. Pink satin ribbon ¼" wide, 12". Small safety pin.

DIRECTIONS: Read General Directions for Little Kitten Baby Accessories. Cut one 15½" × 21½" piece from batting and two from light blue fabric, for front and back. Cut one 1¾" × 15" light blue casing strip and two 6" × 21" gingham pockets. Cut appliqué pieces from fabric as for bath towel.

Place light blue front piece with long edges at sides. Appliqué and embroider cat to front piece as for hand towel, centered between sides and with tips of ears 1¼" below top edge.

For each pocket, fold one long edge of gingham strip ¼", then again ½", to wrong side; press. Topstitch near inner fold, for elastic casing. Cut elastic in half. Using safety pin, thread each half through one casing; tack elastic ends at each end of casing. Baste along remaining long edge and gather to 15½". Pin one pocket piece across organizer front with right sides facing, so that gathered edge is 7¼" above bottom edge of front piece and elastic edge is near bottom. Sew gathered edge to front, ¼" from raw edge. Fold pocket up and pin to front piece with side edges even. Pin second pocket to front piece, right side up and matching bottom and side edges.

For upper casing, fold each short edge of light blue casing strip ½" to wrong side; topstitch. Fold one long casing edge ¼" to wrong side; press. Pin casing to one shorter edge of organizer back piece, centered between sides and with long raw edge even with top edge of back piece. Place back and front pieces together with right sides facing and edges even; place batting piece on top. Sew all around edges, making ¼" seam and leaving an opening at bottom edge for turning. Turn organizer right side out; fold raw edges in and slip-stitch opening closed.

Distribute pocket gathers evenly, then machine-stitch across each elastic casing at vertical center of organizer, forming two openings for each pocket. Cut pink ribbon in half; tie two bows and tack one over each stitching line on elastic casing. Sew a ring at each upper corner on organizer back; insert wood strip in back casing.

Cat and Mouse

Companionable cats and mice are joined by hearts in this cuddly patchwork quilt any youngster would enjoy.

SIZE: 35″ × 53½″.

EQUIPMENT: Ruler. Tape measure. Pencil. Scissors. Paper for patterns. Embroidery and sewing needles. Dressmaker's tracing (carbon) paper. Dry ball-point pen. Small embroidery hoop.

MATERIALS: Closely woven cotton fabrics 44″ wide: white, ¾ yard; pink flowered, ½ yard; gold dotted, ⅞ yard; blue flowered, ⅛ yard; solid pink, ⅛ yard; purple, ¼ yard; pink striped, 1¾ yards. Matching sewing threads. Fiberfill. Quilt batting. Six-strand embroidery floss: brown, white, gold, green, light gray, pale pink, bright pink, blue, purple. Pale pink ribbon ¼″ wide, 1⅛ yards.

DIRECTIONS: Background: Cut fifteen blocks 8½″ square, seven from white fabric and eight from pink flowered fabric. Cut twenty-six strips 1¾″ wide from gold dotted fabric, six 29½″ long and

twenty 8½" long. Lay blocks out in five horizontal rows of three blocks each, alternating colors throughout. In each horizontal row, place a short strip at beginning and end of row and between blocks. With right sides facing and making ¼" seams, join blocks and strips. Place a long strip at top and bottom and between rows; join in same manner to make 29½" × 48" background piece.

Appliqués and Embroidery: Enlarge patterns by copying on paper ruled in ½" squares; complete half patterns indicated by dash lines. Heavy lines indicate appliqués and quilting (small heart), light lines embroidery. Using dressmaker's carbon and dry ball-point pen, transfer following appliqué patterns with embroidery to fabric, leaving ½" between pieces: four cats, four complete mice, and two mouse fronts to white; five cats to blue print; two complete mice and four mouse fronts to solid pink; twenty-four large hearts (with flowers) to purple. (**Note:** Place each mouse or cat in same direction or reverse some patterns to alternate direction if desired.) Do not cut out pieces.

Using embroidery hoop and three strands of floss

in needle, embroider as follows (see embroidery stitch details on page 74): Cats—faces in outline stitch, using gray for eyes and whiskers, light pink for mouths and noses. Mice—ears and whiskers in gray outline stitch, mouths in brown outline stitch, eyes and noses in brown French knots (three for eyes, one for nose); flowers on fronts in gold French knot centers, bright pink lazy daisy petals, green outline stitch stems and green lazy daisy leaves. Hearts—same as mouse fronts, using white for petals.

Review "How to Appliqué," page 75. Following directions for hand appliqué, cut and prepare pieces; appliqué mouse fronts to mice, contrasting colors. Following color illustration, pin a figure in each block 1½" above bottom, alternating mice and cats in each row and contrasting white and colors. Set hearts aside. Using matching thread, baste and slip-stitch appliqués in place, inserting a bit of fiberfill padding under bodies as you baste. Using purple on pink blocks and blue on white blocks, outline each cat or mouse in outline stitch. On white blocks, embroider three or four flowers on either side of cat or mouse in same colors as for mouse fronts (see pattern). For bows, cut pink ribbon into nine pieces 3½″ long and nine pieces ¾″ long. Fold each long piece twice so ends meet in back; tack at center. Wrap a short piece around center, tacking in back. Tack a bow to neck of each cat. For quilting pattern, transfer two small hearts to upper half of each block.

Assembling Quilt: From pink striped fabric, cut piece 42″ × 60½″, for lining and border. Cut batting 35″ × 53½″. Lay lining flat, wrong side up. Center batting on lining, leaving 3½″ margin all around, and baste in place. Center quilt top over batting, leaving 2¾″ margin of batting all around; baste lengthwise, crosswise, and diagonally. Using matching thread, quilt around each figure and on each marked heart (see quilting stitch detail on page 74).

Finishing: Turn in lining edges ½″ and press. At sides of quilt, turning lining to front, covering batting and ¼″ of stripping to make 3″-wide border; topstitch in place. Repeat at top and bottom of quilt, slip-stitching closed at sides.

Appliqué purple hearts as shown; embroider herringbone stitch around each heart, varying colors as desired. Transfer small heart sixteen times around border, centering each one beside a block; quilt.

Snacktime Treats

The quilted ABC wall hanging and dimensional fabric car toy are sunny additions to brighten child's room or after-school snack area. Be ready with milk and cookies!

SIZES: Wall hanging, 21″ × 31½″ plus hanging loops; car toy, 16″ long.

EQUIPMENT: Pencil. Ruler. Paper for patterns. Dressmaker's tracing (carbon) paper. Dry ball-point pen. Scissors. Straight pins. Sewing, quilting, and embroidery needles. Zigzag sewing machine. Iron.

MATERIALS: Closely woven cotton or cotton blend fabrics 45″ wide (see individual directions for colors and amounts). Matching sewing thread. Additional materials as indicated in individual directions.

GENERAL DIRECTIONS: Review "Quilting Compendium," pages 69–76. Prewash all-cotton

1 square = 1 inch

fabric to preshrink; let dry; press. Draw lines across patterns, connecting grid lines. To enlarge for wall hanging, copy onto paper ruled in 1″ squares. Complete half patterns as indicated by long dash lines. Heavy lines indicate pattern outlines; fine lines indicate embroidery. To enlarge pattern for car toy, copy car onto paper ruled in 2″ squares. Appliqué projects by hand or by machine as indicated in individual directions, using matching thread.

WALL HANGING

ADDITIONAL MATERIALS: Fabrics: red, 1 yard; blue denim, ⅜ yard; ¼ yard each of yellow calico, two different navy calicoes, red calico, light blue calico; scraps of green calico, yellow, white. Jumbo rickrack, 12″ lengths of red and yellow. Six-strand embroidery floss, small amounts of black, white, red. Quilt batting. Dowel or bamboo rod, 24″ long, painted red if desired.

DIRECTIONS: Review "Quilting Compendium," pages 69–76. Cut the following rectangles (seam allowance is included in measurements): one 22″×32½″ each from red fabric and batting; one 2½″×24″ and two 15″×11½″ from red fabric; one 15″×11½″ from blue denim; one 8″×11½″ from yellow calico and each navy calico. Set aside first two pieces for lining and hanging loops. Using enlarged patterns and adding ¼″ seam allowance all around, cut appliqués: letters A and C from red, B from denim blue; apple from red calico, leaf and stem from green calico; boat hull from navy calico, first-story cabin from yellow calico, second-story cabin from light blue calico, and smokestack from yellow; car body from light blue calico, windows from white, wheels from navy calico, hub caps from yellow calico.

Appliqué: Referring to photograph for background colors, pin appliqués to center of remaining rectangles, overlapping shapes slightly: Place apple over leaf and stem; work boat from top to bottom, overlapping each previous level; start with car body, layer windows and wheels, then hub caps, on top. Appliqué all pieces by hand. Center red rickrack below boat, yellow rickrack below car; slip-stitch to backgrounds along all edges.

Embroidery: Using dressmaker's carbon and dry ball-point pen, transfer portholes to boat hull, spiraling line of smoke to background. Using three strands of embroidery floss in needle and referring to stitch details on page 74, work red portholes in satin stitch, white smoke in outline stitch. Also work around apple with black in blanket stitch.

Assembly: With right sides facing and making ½″ seams, stitch each letter rectangle to a picture rectangle as shown, A and C to the left, B to the right. Press seams open. In same manner, stitch sections together to front of hanging, which should measure 22″×32½″.

For hanging loops, fold 2½″×24″ strip of red fabric in half lengthwise and wrong side out, and stitch ¼″ from long raw edge. Turn strip to right side; press with seam centered along back. Cut strip into four equal lengths. Fold each piece in half crosswise and pin to front of hanging, one ½″ from each corner, the others centered between, with all raw edges even. Place batting on a large flat surface, with red lining and hanging on top, right sides facing and enclosing loops. Smooth and pin. Machine-stitch around, ½″ from edges, leaving 10″ along bottom edge unstitched. Clip corners, trim batting close to seam, and turn to right side. Press from back. Turn edges under ½″ along opening, and slip-stitch closed.

Quilting: Working from the center outward, baste through all layers in all directions to keep layers from shifting. Using red thread, handquilt around all appliqués. Also quilt around each background rectangle, ¼″ and again 1″ from seams.

Remove basting threads; insert dowel or bamboo rod through hanging loops.

CAR TOY

ADDITIONAL MATERIALS: Fabrics: light blue calico, ½ yard; navy calico, ⅛ yard; scraps of yellow calico and white. Fusible webbing. Polyester fiberfill.

DIRECTIONS: Using enlarged pattern and adding ⅜″ seam allowance all around, cut two car bodies from light blue calico and eight wheels from navy calico. Without adding seam allowance, cut two sets of windows from white fabric, four hub caps from yellow calico, and a piece of fusible webbing for each. Also cut a 2¾″×42″ strip from light blue calico for gusset. Fuse car windows to car body as shown in color photograph; fuse hubcaps to four wheel shapes. Zigzag-stitch around edges. Join the following pieces, right sides facing, edges even and making ⅜″ seams: Place each hub-capped wheel together with a plain wheel; leave 2″ unstitched. Stitch one long edge of gusset around one car body piece, starting at back end of car, turning ends under, and overlapping. Stitch other long edge to second body piece; leave a 5″ opening and turn. Stuff each wheel flatly and evenly; stuff car body plumply. Slip-stitch openings closed. Tack two wheels to each side of car body.

Garden Bunnies

This appliqué crib quilt, with its appealing combination of bunnies and tulips, is cozy enough for baby to use and pretty enough to hang on a wall. Its pieced petaled border creates a unique effect.

SIZE: Approximately 38" square.

MATERIALS: Cotton fabrics 44" wide: off-white, 2½ yards (includes backing); blue and navy prints, 1¼ yards each; ecru print, ⅜ yard. Blue and white sewing thread. Fusible web. Batting.

DIRECTIONS: Read "Quilting Compendium," pages 69–76.

Quilt Blocks: From blue print, mark and cut nine 8" squares, adding seam allowance. Enlarge patterns

for appliqués on a 1" grid. (Heavy lines indicate cutting lines; fine lines indicate machine embroidery.) Transfer to right side of fabrics and cut out, cutting a matching piece for each from fusible web: from ecru, two of each bunny and fifteen tulip heads; from navy blue, five leaf-and-stems pieces. Position either a bunny or a unit composed of a leaf-and-stems piece plus three tulip heads on each square, keeping inside seam allowances. Fuse. Using blue thread and a medium-width zigzag stitch,

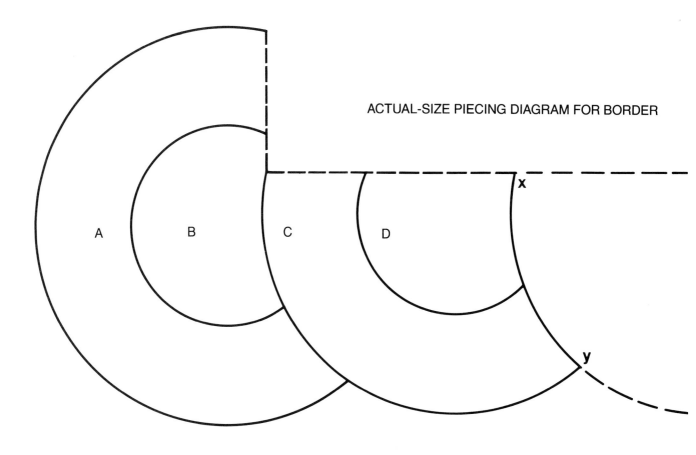

machine-appliqué. Also, machine-embroider along marked lines.

Quilt Top: From off-white fabric, cut joining strips 1½″ wide, adding seam allowance; six 8″ long, four 27″ long, and two 30″ long. Arrange quilt blocks in three rows of three, with tulips at center and corners, bunnies looking straight ahead at top and bottom, and bunnies looking back at sides. Pin, then stitch shortest joining strips between blocks in each row. Pin, then stitch two of next longest strips between rows and the remaining two at sides of quilt top. Stitch longest strips across top and bottom. Quilt top should measure 30″ square inside seam allowances.

From navy fabric, cut 1½″-wide strips: two 30″ long, two 33″ long. Pin, then stitch shorter strips to sides of quilt top, longer strips across top and bottom.

Pieced Border: Piecing diagram is shown actual size; trace patterns for A, B, C, and D, and make templates. From both blue and navy fabrics, cut two A, twenty-four C. From off-white fabric, cut four B, and forty-eight D. Stay-stitch the stitching line on inner curves of A's and C's, and clip. Pin a B to each A and a D to each C. Stitch, then press seam allowance toward darker fabric. Working from right to left, arrange four rows of twelve C-D pieces. Start with a blue C on two of the rows, a navy C on other two; alternate C colors across. With straight edges of D's flush, pin and stitch pieces in each row together between points X and Y as shown on piecing diagram. Each row should measure 31½″ long inside seam allowances on straight edge. Join an A-B unit to the X-Y end of each row, alternating colors.

Pin a row beginning with a blue C along left side of quilt; match top corner of quilt with right edge of (first) C patch, and stop at seam allowance at next corner of quilt, leaving A-B patch loose. Turn quilt clockwise a quarter turn. Pin, then stitch a row along bottom edge in same manner as before, beginning with a navy C piece. Repeat for right side and across top of quilt, alternating starting colors of C's. Fit A-B patches to C's at corners as shown in piecing diagram, turning seam allowance on overlapping C edges under and slip-stitching in place.

Assembly: Cut backing from blue pin dot and batting slightly larger than bordered quilt top. Center quilt top on backing, right sides facing, with batting underneath. Machine-stitch all around, stitching smoothly along curves and reinforcing their intersecting points; leave four adjacent C-D pieces

PATTERNS FOR APPLIQUÉS

1 square = 1 inch

on bottom edge unstitched. Trim backing and batting even with quilt top and clip curves; turn to right side and slip-stitch opening closed. Smooth quilt and press the edge of each scallop. Pin layers together to keep them from shifting.

Quilt by Hand: Using blue thread, quilt around each appliquéd shape, just to the outside of zigzag stitching. Stitch each quilt block on the seam. Stitch the seams of navy borders. Stitch on seams of each B and D patch. Finally, stitch all around quilt, ¼″ from edges.

Quilt Block Fun

Quilt blocks can be used in the variety of ways shown here to create colorful accessories for your home. Choose among the four coordinating quilt blocks in the wall hanging to make the ruffled accent pillow or seat cushion. Youngsters are sure to enjoy playing with a set of puffy soft-sculpture puzzle blocks.

SIZES: Wall hanging, 24″ square. Pillow, 13″ square, plus ruffle. Chair seat pad, 13″ square. Blocks, 2½″ cubes.

EQUIPMENT: Pencil. Graph paper. Ruler. Scissors. Cardboard. Glue. Straight pins. Sewing machine. Sewing needle. Iron. **For Puzzle Block Box:** Hot glue gun (optional).

MATERIALS: Closely woven cotton or cotton-blend, small-print fabrics 45″ wide (see individual directions for colors and amounts). Matching sewing threads. Quilt batting. Additional materials as indicated below.

WALL HANGING

ADDITIONAL MATERIALS: Print fabrics: ¼ yard dark blue; ⅛ yard each medium and light blue, light brown, two medium browns, two roses, pink. Muslin 36″ wide, 1 yard. Wooden dowel ⅜″ diameter, 25½″ long. Two blue wooden 1″ beads. Glue.

DIRECTIONS: Hanging is made up of four patchwork blocks, each assembled with same-size square and triangle patches.

Templates: To make templates for patches, mark patterns on graph paper: A—Mark a 2½″ square. B—Mark a 2½″ square, then divide it in half diagonally for triangle. Do not cut out patterns but glue to graph paper; let dry. Cut on marked lines for templates A and B.

Patches: Following directions below, use templates A and B to make all patches for blocks I, II, III, and IV (see diagrams). For each patch, place template on wrong side of fabric and mark around with pencil held at an outward angle. Mark all patches needed of one color at one time, then cut out each patch ¼″ beyond marked line, which will be stitching line.

Block I: From light brown and dark blue fabrics, cut four each of A and eight each of B.

Block II: From pink fabric, cut four of A and eight of B. From rose and one of the medium brown fabrics, cut eight of B.

Block III: From rose and medium blue fabrics, cut eight each of A.

Block IV: From another medium brown fabric, cut eight of A and eight of B. From light blue fabric, cut eight of B.

Blocks: To begin sewing each block, match each B patch with another B patch of contrasting color, as shown in diagrams; join B's on their long edges with ¼″ seams to make B squares. Join A and B squares to make two-patch rows. Join rows to make four-patch blocks. Join four blocks to make the finished block. Each finished block should measure 10½″ square, including seam allowance around edges.

Assembling: From muslin, cut three strips 1½″ wide: two 10½″ long, one 21½″ long. Lay out the four blocks in two rows in order shown. Place a 10½″ strip between blocks in each horizontal row and join to blocks with ¼″ seam. Place 21½″ strip between rows and join. Piece should measure 21½″ square. From muslin cut four strips 1¾″ wide: two 21½″ long and two 24″ long. Join 21½″ strips to sides of piece, then 24″ strips to top and bottom. Piece should measure 24″ square.

Quilting: Cut 24″ squares from muslin and batting. Smooth batting over muslin, then center patchwork on top. Pin, then baste to keep layers from shifting. Machine-quilt, starting from the center and working outward; stitch close to seams connecting patches of two contrasting fabrics, thus outlining each color area. Also quilt around each block close to seam joining muslin strips.

Binding: From dark blue print, cut 2⅛″-wide strips and piece for 100″ length. Press under one long edge ½″, the other edge ⅝″. Fold strip in half lengthwise with pressed edges inside. Open out the ½″ turn under and, starting at a corner, pin along quilt top, right sides facing, matching raw edges, and mitering corners; stitch with ½″ seam. Turn binding to back of quilt; pin. Topstitch from front, securing binding to both sides of quilt.

Hanging Loops: Cut four 1½″ × 3″ strips. Turn all edges under ¼″ and fold in half lengthwise; topstitch along all edges. Fold in half crosswise and pin ends to back of quilt, spaced evenly along top edge; stitch. Place dowel through loops and glue a bead onto each dowel end.

PILLOW

ADDITIONAL MATERIALS: Print fabrics: ⅛ yard each medium brown, light blue, and dark blue. Muslin 36″ wide, ⅜ yard. Ecru pregathered eyelet trim with bound edge, 1½″ wide, 1½ yards. Polyester fiberfill.

DIRECTIONS: Referring to directions for Wall Hanging, make templates A and B; cut patches for and assemble Block IV. From muslin, cut four 1¾″-wide border strips, two 10½″ long and two 13″ long. Make ¼″ seams, join 10½″ and two 13″ long. Making ¼″ seams, join 10½″ strips to top and bottom of block; join 13″ strips to side. Pillow top should measure 13″ square. Cut 13″ squares of muslin and batting. Layer pillow top over batting and muslin; baste and quilt as for Wall Hanging.

From muslin, cut two rectangles, one 11″ × 13″, another 6″ × 13″. On each rectangle, turn under one 13″ edge ¼″ twice; stitch. Overlap finished edges and pin to form a 13″ square for pillow backing. Pin backing to patchwork pillow top, wrong sides facing. Stitch all around, ⅜″ from raw edges.

From dark blue print, cut 2⅛″-wide strips and piece for 55″ length. Bind edges as for Wall Hanging. Cut 55″ length of eyelet. Place around pillow front with bound edge resting on blue binding and ruffle extending beyond binding. With ecru thread in needle and blue thread in bobbin, topstitch all around eyelet binding, mitering corners and overlapping ends.

Make pillow form: Cut two 14″ squares from muslin; pin together and stitch around with ½″ seam, leaving opening in one side. Clip corners; turn to right side. Stuff plumply with fiberfill; turn in edges of opening ½″ and slip-stitch closed. Insert pillow form from back of pillow.

CHAIR SEAT PAD

ADDITIONAL MATERIALS: Print fabrics: ¼ yard dark blue; ⅛ yard light brown. Muslin 36″ wide, ⅜ yard. Ecru ribbon ⅜″ wide, ⅝ yard. Polyester fiberfill.

DIRECTIONS: Make as for pillow, using Block I. As you join pieced front to back, round the two corners to be placed at chair front. Omit eyelet trim. For inner pillow, use less fiberfill and stuff flatly and evenly. Cut ribbon in half; tack center of each half to a back corner of seat pad.

BLOCK I

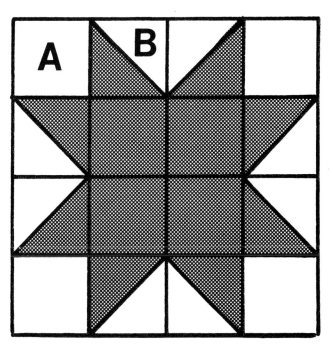

BLOCK II

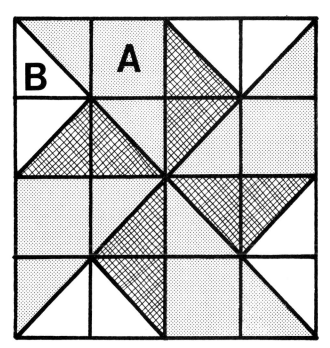

BLOCK III

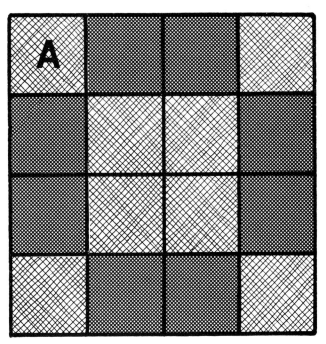

BLOCK IV

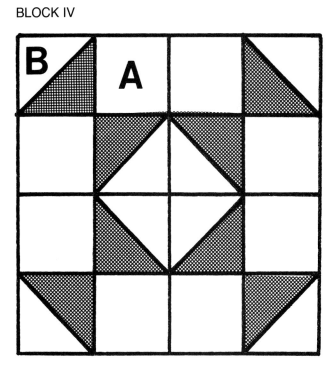

 Browns

Pink

Blues

Roses

PUZZLE BLOCKS

ADDITIONAL MATERIALS: Print fabrics: ⅛ yard of each color listed for Wall Hanging. Muslin 36″ wide, ⅛ yard. Polyester fiberfill. Wooden slats ¼″ thick, two 2″×10″, two 2″×10½″. Masonite ¼″ thick, 10″ square. Wood glue or hot melt glue.

DIRECTIONS: Referring to directions for Wall Hanging, make templates A and B. Cut all patches for each of the four blocks. Join B triangles to make B squares. Cut thirty-two additional A squares, sixteen from muslin and sixteen from a blue print. There should now be a total of ninety-six squares.

Setting aside the additional A squares, lay out patches to make the four block designs. Put one design on top of another in order, and follow it with third and fourth designs, piling the squares neatly and evenly. Now put on a muslin layer, then a blue layer, covering each top square. Each pile will form one cubic block; pin each pile to avoid confusion.

Sew each cube as follows: Join first two squares along one edge. Beginning at end of seam just made, join adjacent edges of third square to top edges of first two. Repeat with three more squares. Pin both threesomes together to form a cube; stitch all but one edge. Clip corners; turn to right side. Stuff plumply with fiberfill, and turn open edges ¼″ to inside. Slip-stitch closed.

Box: Glue ends of 10″ slats to sides of 10½″ slats to form a square frame. Glue masonite inside back of frame for bottom of box. Place blocks in box. Use blocks to form each patchwork design in turn or to create new designs.

QUILTING COMPENDIUM

While all of the quilting projects in this book feature complete how-to instructions, this section will serve as a reference for the quilting, appliqué, and embroidery techniques common to all or many of the individual projects.

TOOLS AND EQUIPMENT

Begin by gathering tools and equipment before starting your quilting projects. Normally, there are five different steps involved in making a quilt; each step along the way requires special tools or equipment. Materials to have on hand for pattern-making include mechanical pencil, transparent or metal rulers, white paper, tracing vellum, clear tape, fine-tip black marker, drafting triangles, protractor, compass, and a pair of good-quality sharp scissors.

Equipment that you would use to make templates include graph paper (eight squares to the inch); Aleene's "Tacky" glue; thin, stiff cardboard or fine sandpaper; quilter's gridded template plastic; craft knife with extra blades; and a wooden cutting board.

For cutting and sewing the parts of the quilt, you'll need a tape measure, yardstick, tailor's chalk, water-erasable marking pencil, straight pins, dressmaker's shears, rotary cutter and cutting mat, sewing needles, beeswax, zigzag sewing machine with a zipper foot, steam iron, ironing board, and a press cloth.

If the quilt requires embroidery you'll need embroidery scissors, embroidery needles, tapestry needles, colored pencils, and optional embroidery hoop or frame.

SELECTING MATERIALS

Fabric
Select fabrics that are closely woven, so seams will hold and edges won't fray. Fabrics should be fairly soft. Avoid fabrics so thin that seam allowances will show through. Wash and dry new cotton or cotton-blend fabrics to preshrink them and remove any sizing. Yardages given are for preshrunk fabric; *buy 2 to 5 percent extra to allow for shrinkage.* Press all fabrics smooth

Thread
Use a good quality mercerized cotton or cotton-covered polyester thread for piecing and appliqué work. Use 100-percent cotton quilting thread whenever possible when hand-quilting. Run each strand of thread across a cake of beeswax to strengthen it.

Batting
Most batting is made from either polyester, cotton, or wool. Polyester is most commonly used, as it holds together better, does not lump, and will dry quickly when the quilt is washed. Polyester batting should be bonded, glazed, or needlepunched to prevent "bearding" (fibers migrating through the fabric to the quilt top). Cotton and wool battings are more comfortable to sleep under, as they "breathe," and can give a more traditional look to a quilt. They are easier to quilt through but also need to be quilted more closely (lines not more than 2″ apart), so that the batting does not shift. Dry-cleaning is generally recommended for quilts filled with natural batting.

Antique quilts with close, ornate quilting designs require cotton or low-loft polyester batting to facilitate and showcase fine quilting. Designs with a minimum of quilting can be made with high-loft batting. Needlepunched or bonded batting is best for machine quilting and for strip-piecing directly onto batting. Alternatives to batting include a wool blanket or several layers of preshrunk cotton flannel.

MAKING PATTERNS

Patterns given are either reduced on a grid or printed actual size. Half and quarter patterns are indicated by long dash lines at their center edge(s). Trace actual-size patterns. Enlarge patterns from a grid as directed below, using a ruler to make straight lines. When one pattern has been superimposed on another, make separate patterns. Complete half and quarter patterns, unless otherwise directed.

Enlarging Patterns

Using a ruler and mechanical pencil, draw lines across the pattern, connecting grid lines (Figures 1, 2). Count the number of boxes along both edges of the pattern. Draw the same number of boxes on a sheet of paper (Figure 3), making boxes the size indicated on the pattern.

Begin at box in upper left corner of grid. In our example, there are no pattern lines in any box of Row 1, so proceed to the fourth box of Row 2. Draw pattern lines on the paper: Box by box, copy pat-

tern lines and markings to look the same way enlarged on your paper as they do on the original pattern. This method can be done more quickly by taping translucent paper over a pattern cutting board ruled with 1″ squares (if the grid is labeled 1 square = 1″).

Other methods of enlarging include: 1. Having a photostat made. 2. Using a photocopier with an enlarger (you may have to piece large patterns together afterwards). 3. Using an opaque projector at a local school or library. 4. Using slide film to take a head-on photo, projecting it to the size needed, then tracing it onto paper.

Figure 1

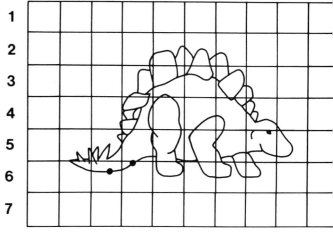

Figure 2

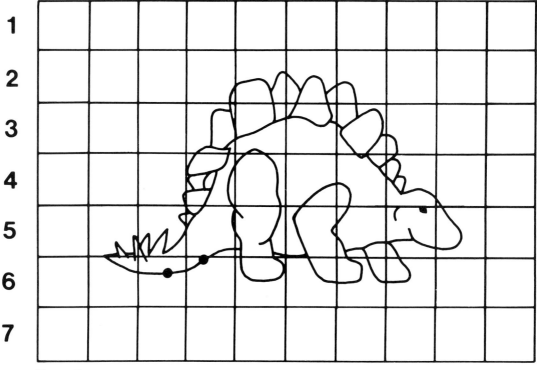

Figure 3

Completing Half Patterns

Trace pattern twice on vellum. Turn one copy over, then tape tracings together at dash lines (Figure 4). If desired, use another sheet of tracing vellum to trace completed pattern.

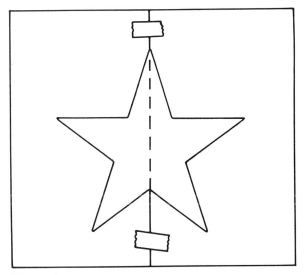

Figure 4

Making Templates

Trace actual-size patterns, or draft patterns onto graph paper, following dimensions given. Use a compass for circles. Glue patterns to cardboard or sandpaper; let glue dry before cutting out *just inside marked lines*. Or, draw or trace patterns directly on gridded template plastic. Replace much-used templates before they begin to fray.

Take care to make templates accurately so that pieces will fit together properly. Pretest them by using them to draw the entire quilt block, referring to diagrams given; make adjustments if necessary.

Transferring Patterns

For thin or light-colored fabrics: Trace pattern; darken lines with black marker. Tape pattern, with white paper beneath, to work surface. Tape fabric on top, then trace with water-erasable pencil. Or, tape pattern and fabric to a glass door, window, or table with light source on opposite side.

For quilting motifs, make a plastic or cardboard template: Cut pencil-width slots (similar to a stencil) for each line, breaking slots as necessary. Lay template on quilt top and mark through slots with water-erasable pencil or chalk. Complete lines as necessary.

Perforated templates can also be used for quilting motifs. To make one, transfer motifs onto strong paper, such as Kraft paper or an office file folder. Hand prick at ⅛" intervals with a darning needle,

or use a sewing machine equipped with a #16 or #18 *unthreaded* needle set at longest stitch length. If necessary, rub underside of template with fine sandpaper to open holes completely. Place perforated pattern on right side of fabric in desired position. Using a soft cloth, rub powder through the holes: Use cornstarch or French chalk for dark fabrics, and cinnamon or cocoa for light fabrics. Remove pattern; join powder dots with a water-erasable pencil or chalk. Remove powder from fabric.

CUTTING

Pull a thread across width of fabric to determine grain; cut along thread. Lay fabric flat, wrong side up. Read through all directions given and set aside fabric for lining, borders, and binding *before* marking patches. Do not cut border or binding pieces until directed.

Squares and oblongs must be placed with the weave of the fabric parallel to edges. Diamond-shaped patches need two sides on straight of the fabric. Right-angle triangles may be cut with two sides on the straight of the goods. For tumbler shapes, the half pattern should be cut with the fold on the straight of the fabric.

Mark pieces starting with the largest patches. Using light-colored pencil on dark fabric and dark-colored pencil on light fabric, trace around template, holding pencil at an outward angle so that its point is firmly against the template edge. When tracing a number of pieces on one fabric, leave space between pieces for seam allowances. For patches and appliqué pieces, you will need ¼" seam allowance all around each one. **Note:** Yardage requirements in this book are based on careful placement of pattern on fabric. Unless otherwise indicated, patterns should be placed leaving ½" between two pieces—this will give you the full ¼" seam allowance that is necessary for each.

SEWING

Seaming

Pin or baste pieces, having right sides together and raw edges even. Machine-stitch with matching thread, making ¼"-wide seams, unless otherwise directed. Ease in fullness where necessary. Press piecing seams to one side, generally toward the darker fabric, unless otherwise directed (seams pressed open may weaken your project). As you piece and press, clip seam allowances at curves; trim seam allowances at corners and wherever else necessary.

Making Split Squares

This speed technique is useful when a large number of squares, each composed of two contrasting triangles, are required.

From the project directions, calculate the number of split squares required. Divide this number in half to determine the number of squares to mark. (For example, if twenty-four finished squares are required, twelve need to be marked.)

Add seam allowance to the desired finished size of the square: *This is always ⅞".* (For example, the finished square size is 1½", so the marked square size is 2⅜".) For 1" squares, mark 1⅞" ones; for 2", mark 2⅞" ones, etc.

Arrange the squares to be marked into a shape as close to a square as possible. (For twelve, mark three squares by four squares.) Multiply these numbers by the calculated square size to give the fabric dimensions needed. (For our example, $3 \times 2⅜ = 7⅛"$; $4 \times 2⅜ = 9½"$. Cut one piece of each fabric 7⅛" × 9½".)

Stack fabrics with right sides together. Hand-baste layers together thoroughly. Using ruler and water-erasable pencil, mark squares (see diagram). Draw one set of diagonals (final cutting line) across all squares. Draw seam lines ¼" to either side of previous lines (shown as dash lines on diagram).

Stitch along all marked seam lines, then cut along all remaining marked lines. Remove the few stitches holding points of corners together. Open squares out flat; press seam allowances toward darkest square.

Split Squares Diagram

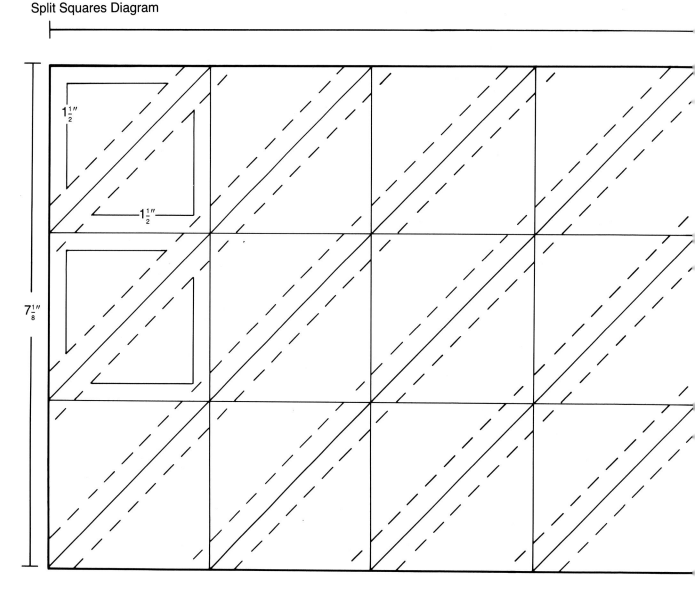

Joining Diamonds or Hexagons

To keep angles sharp and seams precise, prepare a paper liner for each piece: Cut a firm paper pattern from Kraft, freezer, or shelf paper the exact size of your template. Fit this paper liner within marked outline on wrong side of patch. Hold patch with the liner uppermost. Press seam allowance over each side and tack to the paper with one stitch on each edge, allowing the thread to cross corners; finish by tacking an extra stitch on the first side. Cut thread, leaving a short tail. To make removal of tacking easier, do not knot the thread or make any backstitches. Hold prepared patches right sides together, matching edges to be seamed. Whipstitch edges together with fine, even stitches, avoiding catching in the paper liners. Keep liners in place until quilt top is complete, then snip tacking threads and remove them.

Assembling Quilt Top

As you work, measure each unit—blocks, rows, etc.—to make sure it is of equal size to previous units. Compare your measurements with those given in the directions and make any adjustments necessary. Our measurements are strictly mathematical and do not allow for the variance that can result from multiple piecing. *If necessary, adjust dimensions of borders, batting, and lining to fit your project.*

To Miter Corners

Stitch borders to quilt top, with an equal length extending at each side of the quilt. Lay quilt top flat, right side down. Hold adjacent ends of border pieces at corners with right sides facing. Keeping border flat, lift up inner corners and pin strips together diagonally from inner corner to outer corner. Use 45-degree drafting triangle or transparent ruler to check straightness of pins. Baste, then stitch on final basting line. Trim fabric ¼" from stitching; press seam open.

Making a Pillow

Make pillow front as directed; cut pillow back the same size. Add ruffle, piping, or other trims if directed, then assemble pillow: Stitch front and back together, making ½" seams (unless otherwise directed), and leaving an opening along bottom edge for turning. Turn pillow right side out. Stuff firmly with fiberfill, or insert pillow form. Turn in raw edges and slip-stitch closed.

For Ruffle

Cut fabric strip, piecing as necessary. Stitch short ends together; press seam open. Fold and press strip in half lengthwise, right side out. Using a long basting stitch, gather ½" from raw edges to fit around pillow. Stitch to right side of pillow front.

Preparing Fabric

To prevent fabric from raveling, overcast edges by hand or zigzag by machine. To mark center of fabric, baste across piece in both directions with contrasting thread. If desired, work embroidery in a hoop or frame to keep fabric taut; move hoop as needed.

Embroidering

Cut floss into 18" lengths. Separate six-strand floss or Persian-type yarn and work with designated number of strands in needle. Begin embroidery by leaving a tail on back and working over it to secure. To end a strand or to begin a new one, weave under wrong side of stitches; do not make knots unless directed. Referring to photo and chart or pattern, work designs as directed, following color key, if any. Refer to illustrated stitch details (page 74) as needed. Stitching tends to twist the working strand; occasionally allow needle and strand to hang freely from work to untwist. When moving from one area of design to another, do not carry colors across wrong side of work, as they may show through on right side.

Working Counted Cross-Stitch

Each symbol on a chart represents one cross-stitch worked over one "square" of fabric, unless otherwise directed. Different symbols represent different colors. Solid lines represent straight stitches or backstitches. Large dots represent French knots.

Using a colored pencil, draw intersecting lines across the chart to mark its center. Work design, matching center of the fabric to center of the chart. Thread tapestry needle with number of strands of floss indicated. Work cross-stitches first, then any additional embroidery. When working cross-stitches, work all underneath stitches in one direction and all the top stitches in the opposite direction; make sure all strands lie smooth and flat. Make crosses touch by inserting needle in same hole as adjacent stitch.

Remove basting and water-soluble markings. Steam-press piece face down on a well-padded surface.

Embroidery Stitch Detail

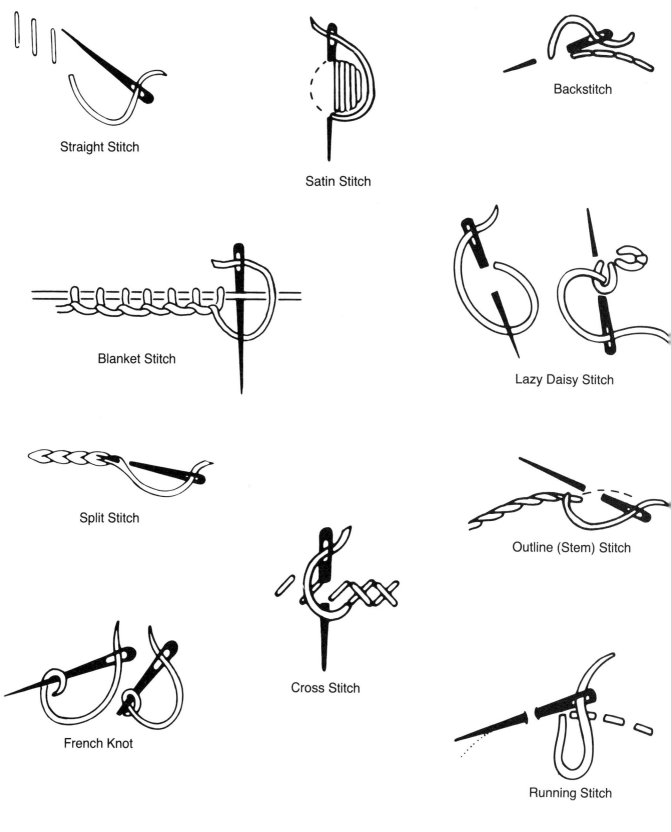

Straight Stitch

Satin Stitch

Backstitch

Blanket Stitch

Lazy Daisy Stitch

Split Stitch

Outline (Stem) Stitch

French Knot

Cross Stitch

Running Stitch

Choose a fabric that is closely woven and firm enough so a clean edge results when the pieces are cut. Cut a pattern piece for each shape out of thin, stiff cardboard, and mark the right side of each pattern piece. Press fabric smooth.

Place cardboard pattern, wrong side up, on wrong side of fabric. Using sharp, hard pencils (light-colored pencil on dark fabric and dark pencil on light fabric), mark the outline on the fabric. When marking several pieces on the same fabric, leave at least ½" between pieces. Mark a second outline ¼" outside the design outline. Using matching thread and small stitches, machine-stitch all around design outline, as shown in Figure 1. This makes edge easier to turn and neater in appearance. Cut out the appliqué on the outside line, as shown in Figure 2. For a smooth edge, clip into seam allowance at curved edges and corners. Then turn seam allowance to back, just inside stitching as shown in Figure 3, and press. (You may prefer to place some pieces so they overlap the raw edges of adjacent pieces; study overall design before turning under edges of all pieces.) Pin and baste the appliqué on the background, and slip-stitch in place with tiny stitches, as shown in Figure 4.

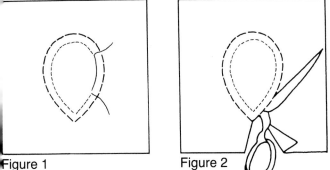

Figure 1   Figure 2

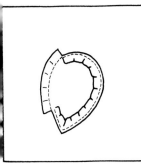
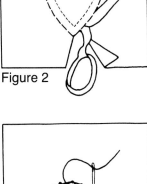

Figure 3   Figure 4

The quilting design is usually marked on the quilt top after the top is completed but before it is joined to the batting and lining. Border designs should be traced around the outside, with all-over quilting in the center of the quilt.

After the quilting design has been marked on the quilt top, assemble top, batting, and lining. Cut or piece lining fabric to equal size of the quilt top. Place lining, wrong side up, on a large flat surface. Place one layer of cotton or Dacron batting on top of the lining, smoothing out any bumps or wrinkles. If the quilt is planned for warmth, the interlining may be thicker. Remember, the thinner the layer of padding, the easier and finer the quilting will be.

Place quilt top right side up on top of batting. Pin all layers together to hold temporarily. Baste generously through all thicknesses. To prevent shifting, first baste on the lengthwise and crosswise grain of the fabric. Then baste diagonally across in two directions and around sides, top, and bottom. **Note:** If quilting is to be done using a quilting hoop, extra care must be taken to keep basting stitches close, so they will hold in place as you change the position of the hoop.

Quilting

Quilting may be done by hand or on the sewing machine.

When quilting by hand, the quilt may be stretched on a frame or in a quilting hoop (more easily handled and movable). If neither frame nor hoop is used, quilting may be done in the lap over small areas at a time.

Quilting Needle and Thread
The usual quilting needle is a short, sharp needle—#8 or #9—although some experienced quilters may prefer a longer one. Strong white sewing thread between #30 and #50 is best.

Tying a Quilter's Knot
Thread your quilting needle with quilting thread about 18" long. Hold the threaded eye between thumb and index finger. Bring thread tail over needle and hold against the needle's eye. Wind thread

over and around the needle three or four times. Pull wound coils over the needle and down the length of the thread until they tighten at the end. Trim thread beyond knot if necessary.

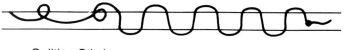

Quilting Stitch

Hand Quilting

Use a quilting frame or hoop if desired. Either is especially helpful if the quilt is large and/or the quilting design is ornate. Tie a quilter's knot, then bring needle through lining, batting, and top at the beginning of the marked line. Tug gently on thread so knot pops through lining and lodges in batting. Keeping left hand underneath the quilt and right hand on top, work a small running stitch along quilting lines. Make stitches as small and even as possible (five to ten per inch). Space stitches evenly, so they are the same length on both sides of quilt. Periodically check the length of stitches on quilt lining.

To end off, make a triple half-hitch knot and pop it through the quilt top, lodging it in a seam allowance or previous row of quilting whenever possible. Or, take two backstitches; on the second stitch, bring the needle 1″ or so through the quilt top and batting only, and cut the thread where it surfaces—the thread end will sink into the batting.

Quilting on a Frame

If a frame is used, sew top and bottom edges of lining to the fabric strips that are attached to the long parallel bars of your quilting frame. Using strong thread so that the quilt will not pull away from the frame when stretched taut, sew securely with several rows of stitches. After the quilt is se-cured in the frame, start quilting midway between the long parallel bars of the frame and sew toward you. Turn to stitch the other side in the same fashion.

Quilting with a Quilting Hoop

Start quilting at the center of the quilt, then work toward outer edges. Pull quilt taut in the hoop and move any extra fullness toward the edges. If necessary, cut basting thread as work progresses. As your quilting comes closer to the edge, smaller embroidery hoops may be substituted for the larger quilting hoop, to make sure that fabric will remain taut.

Machine Quilting

The best patterns to use for machine quilting are those with diagonal lines. Fabric gives a little when on the bias, making it easier to keep the area you are working on flat. Use a straight stitch; set stitch length between six and twelve stitches per inch. Adjust pressure so that it is slightly heavier than for medium-weight fabrics. Use a short-, open-toed quilting foot, if possible. An adjustable space guide arm will help space rows of stitches evenly. For particularly thick quilts, an even-feed or walking foot will help to keep the layers from shifting.

To begin, roll up one half of quilt tightly and place it to the right of needle. Safety pins will help keep the quilt rolled. Begin stitching at the center of the quilt and work to the right, unrolling the quilt as necessary. Turn quilt and repeat for remaining half.

QUILT CARE

Dry clean all fine quilts. If a quilt is washable, you may put it in the automatic washer on a short-wash cycle. Be sure to use only a mild soap or detergent. Do not wring or spin dry. Let quilt drip dry, and do not iron.

SOURCE GUIDE

Write for direct mail-order information or the name of a store near you.

DMC®—Available in needlework shops or by mail from

> Craft Gallery Ltd.
> P.O. Box 145
> Swampscott, MA 01907

For further information, write to:
> DMC
> Port Kearny Building #10
> South Kearny, NJ 07032-0650

Pellon®—Write to or call
> Pellon
> 119 West 40th Street
> New York, NY 10018
> 1-800-223-5275

Velcro®—Write to or call
> Velcro
> P.O. Box 4806
> Manchester, NH 03108
> 1-603-669-4892

Vogart®—Write to or call
> Vogart Crafts Corporation
> 150 Queen Parkway
> West Columbia, SC 29169
> 1-800-237-8001

INDEX

Animal motifs, 14–15, 43–46, 47–53, 54–56, 61–63
Appliqué, 11–13, 24–27, 61–63
  how to, 75
Appliqué Pussycat (quilt), 43–46
Assembling quilt top, 73
Autumn Leaves (quilt), 39–42

Baby, accessories for, 47–69
Bath towel, 47, 51
Batting, 69
Bib, 47–53
Blocks, toy, 64–68
Bookmarks, 24, 27
Bun warmer, 24, 25

Calendar holder, 24, 25
Capture a Snowflake (wall hangings), 16–18
Car toy, 57–60
Cat and Mouse (quilt), 54–56
Chair seat pad, 64–66
Children, accessories for, 47–69
Christmas motif, 16–18
Cookbook marker, 24, 27
Corners, mitering, 73
Country Coordinates (kitchen accessories), 24–27
Crib quilt, 61–63
Cross-stitch, 73
Cutting, 71

Diaper holder, 47, 50, 52
DMC©, 77
Door sign, 47, 51
Dry cleaning, 76
Dustcover, 14

Embroidery, 73
Embroidery stitch detail, 74
Equipment, for quilting, 69

Fabric, 69
  preparing for embroidery, 73
Finishing, 73
Floral motifs, 7–10, 11–13, 24–27, 28–31, 38–42, 61–63
Floral Shadows (accessories), 7–10
Frame, quilted, 7–10
Frame, quilting on, 76

Garden Bunnies (crib quilt), 61–63

Half patterns, 71
Hand quilting, 76
Hand towel, 47, 51
Hoop, quilting, 76

Joining, 73
Junior Attractions, 47–53

Kitchen ensemble, 24–27

Laundering, 76
Little Kitten baby accessories, 47–50

Machine quilting, 76
Mitering corners, 73

Needle, quilting, 75
Nursery Pals (accessories), 47–53

Ohio Star with pinwheel center, 32–34
Ohio Star with triangle border, 32–35

Patchwork, 11
Patterns
enlarging, 70
making, 69–71
transferring, 71
Pellon©, 57
Picture frame, 7–9
Pillows, 28–31, 32–38, 47–53, 64–68
how to make, 73
Pinwheel pillows, 32–33
Place mat, 24, 26–27
Planter, quilted, 7–8
Pot holders, 19–21
Puzzle blocks, 64–68

Quiet rattle, 47, 52
Quilt Block Fun (blocks), 64–68
Quilt care, 76
Quilter's knot, 75
Quilting
history of, 5
shadow, 28
Quilting Compendium, 69–76
Quilts, 32–38, 39–42, 43–46, 47–53, 54–56, 61–63

Radiant Star, 32, 35–36
Rattle, baby's, 47, 52
Red and White Pattern Play (quilt and pillows), 32–38

Ruffles, 28–31, 64–68
how to make, 73

Seaming, 71
Seat cushion, 64, 66–67
Sewing, 71–72
Sewing machine cover, 14–15
Shadow quilting, 28
Sitting Pretty Sewing Machine Cover, 14–15
Snacktime Treats (children's accessories), 57–60
Sources, for equipment and materials, 77
Split squares, 72
Star Flower Table Runner, 11–13
Star motif, 11–13, 32–38, 64–68

Table runner, 11–13
Take Time for Tea (quilt), 19–23
Templates, 71
Thread, 69, 75
Tissue-box cover, 7–10
Tools, for quilting, 69
Tote bag, 7–10
Towels, 47–53
Toys, 64–68

Velcro©, 77
Vogart©, 77

Wall hangings, 16–18, 57–60, 64–68
Wall organizer, 47–53
Washcloth, 47–53
Washing quilts, 76
Wild Goose Chase Quilt, 32–38

All of us at Meredith® Press are dedicated to offering you, our customer, the best books we can create. We are particularly concerned that all of the instructions for making the projects are clear and accurate. We welcome your comments and would like to hear any suggestions you may have. Please address your correspondence to Customer Service Department, Meredith® Press, Meredith Corporation, 150 East 52nd Street, New York, NY 10022.